PRAISE FOR BROKEN CIRCLE

Now an approved curriculum resource for secondary
students in Manitoba and British Columbia.

Fontaine shares his healing journey with grace, insight and respect for where his story ends and another's begins. The opportunities for critical thinking are rich, specifically regarding the complex impact of residential schools on individuals, families, communities and Canada as a nation.

BRITISH COLUMBIA EDUCATIONAL
RESOURCE ACQUISITION CONSORTIUM (ERAC)

Theodore Fontaine has written a testimony that should be mandatory reading for everyone out there who has ever wondered, "Why can't Aboriginal people just get over Residential Schools?" Mr. Fontaine's life story is filled with astonishing and brutal chapters, but, through it all, time, healing, crying, writing, friends and family, and love—sweet love—have all graced their way into the man, father, son, brother, husband, and child of wonder Theodore has always deserved to be. What a humbling work to read. I'm grateful he wrote it and had the courage to share it. *Mahsi cho.*

RICHARD VAN CAMP
Author of *The Moon of Letting Go*

Too many survivors of Canada's Indian residential schools live to forget. Theodore Fontaine writes to remember. It's taken a lifetime to make peace with the pain, shame and fear inflicted upon a little boy wrenched from his family when he was only seven. Ted hasn't forgotten, but he has forgiven. This is what makes his voyage of self-discovery so compelling. This memoir is a life lesson about hope, healing and happiness.

HANA GARTNER
CBC's *The Fifth Estate*

First and foremost, *Broken Circle* is a reflection of Ted's courage. It is also a hopeful, inspirational story that will give courage to other residential school survivors. It will show them that they're not alone and that these unique stories are a part of Canadian history that should be told. Above all, *Broken Circle* is about healing and reconciliation. It makes its point, but there's nothing vindictive about it. Lovely.

Broken Circle takes readers by the hand and walks us through the lonely corridors of Fort Alexander Indian Residential School. Mr. Fontaine discloses how the trauma he suffered as a result of his incarceration in Canada's Indian residential school system has affected him throughout his life. What I find remarkable about his memoir is the generosity, bravery and open-heartedness with which he shares these sometimes joyous, sometimes painful moments of his life. In the spirit of reconciliation, Mr. Fontaine brings us to his own healing. And in this way he has added to the healing of us all.

If you believe, as I do, that knowing our past can help us make positive changes in our future, read this book…[Theodore] is doing a remarkable service for First Nations, but also helping non-Aboriginal people see the destructive impact of residential schools.

BROKEN CIRCLE

BROKEN CIRCLE

The Dark Legacy of
INDIAN RESIDENTIAL SCHOOLS

A Memoir

THEODORE FONTAINE

VICTORIA · VANCOUVER · CALGARY

Heritage House Publishing Company Ltd.
heritagehouse.ca

CATALOGUING INFORMATION AVAILABLE FROM LIBRARY AND ARCHIVES CANADA

978-1-926613-66-6 (pbk)
978-1-926936-06-2 (epub)

EDITORS Jean Wilson and Vivian Sinclair
PROOFREADER Lesley Cameron
COVER AND BOOK DESIGNER Jacqui Thomas
FRONT-COVER PHOTOS Fort Alexander Indian Residential School courtesy of the author; shattered-glass photo by Ejla/iStockphoto
PHOTO INSERT belterz/iStockphoto (photo borders); Photoslash/iStockphoto (background)
ALL OTHER PHOTOS Courtesy of the author unless otherwise noted

This book was produced using FSC®-certified, acid-free paper, processed chlorine free and printed with vegetable-based inks.

We acknowledge the financial support of the Government of Canada through the Canada Book Fund and the Canada Council for the Arts, and the Province of British Columbia through the British Columbia Arts Council and the Book Publishing Tax Credit.

Canada Canada Council Conseil des arts for the Arts du Canada BRITISH COLUMBIA BRITISH COLUMBIA ARTS COUNCIL An agency of the Province of British Columbia

Printed in Canada

20 19 18   7 8 9

For years I suffered in silence. I wondered if other children had to lose their families at age seven or even younger just to attend school. I came to believe that it was natural to be wrenched from your family at this age. I lived with the daily reminder that we were not like the predominant white race. The pounding into our minds that we were less than our keepers took its toll: more than two-thirds of my schoolmates died early, mostly from lives lived trying to forget.

To all my departed schoolmates and to all those who have survived the damage, the indignities, the suffering and the true intent of Indian residential schools, I dedicate this book. We suffered individually but now come together. We are not alone.

In memory of Allan—"Chubby"—my friend and close cousin who left us too early. I owe my healing and my gratitude to your teaching me to talk, to listen and to work to understand the true nature and intent of the Indian residential school system. You made it okay to talk about it. I miss you dearly, Chubby.

To my mom, Margaret, whose innocent, persistent dream was for me and the rest of her children, Cliff, Leon, Marie, Marge and Shirley, to become just as successful as the children of the white ladies she worked for almost daily for over 30 years. As mothers will do, those ladies from the adjacent town of Pine Falls barraged her with stories of their children "doing successful things and having good jobs." As the years went by, she endured in silence the disparaging neighbourhood views and chatter at these homes regarding her people on the reserve, spoken around her as if she was not even there.

Mom, it has been 16 years since you left us and almost 40 years since your youngest child last attended an Indian residential school. We all attained the success you imagined for us, and it brings warmth to feel your loving eyes and smile radiating down on us. In writing this book, you have been at my side with your loving hand on my shoulder, telling your friends all around you, "This is my boy and he has written his story."

To my daughter, Jacqueline, and her husband, Ron, who have loved me through it all and have risen above the damage in my life to achieve success in their marriage and careers, and to bless us with grandsons, Sage and Hudson. It is comforting to know that our two little men can never be taken the way I was so many years ago.

To my wife, Morgan, my incredible partner, the other half of my *niizhota* (double heart, or twoheart). I cannot imagine this little Indian boy opening himself to some of those inner conflicts and hurts without your love, support, courage and laughter. You are my *assin*—my rock.

This book aims to confront the truth and the legacy of Indian residential schools. To those who carry that burden, silently still: it was real, it did happen, and we have survived.

CONTENTS

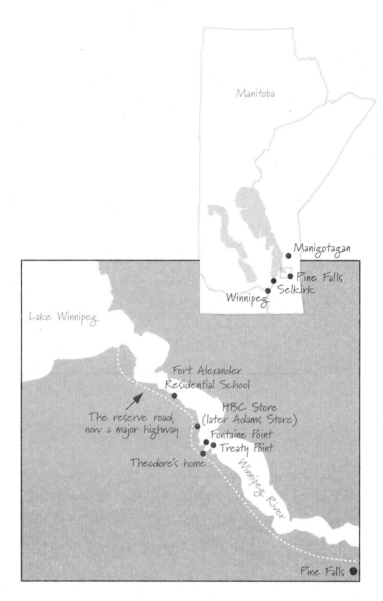

Map of the Fort Alexander area as it was when I was a child.
The residential school was about a mile from my home. My grandfather
Niizhotay trapped in the area around Manitogatan (the missionaries
inaccurately translated the village name as "Bad Throat"). The school
has now been bulldozed.

PREFACE

Early on, I discovered that I could escape from the loneliness and sadness of my life at Indian residential school by recalling and reliving my joyous life as a boy at home before school. It also became apparent early on that I could write the English language better than I could speak it.

In my third or fourth year at school, Mom and the other mothers were allowed to join us in our classrooms on Mother's Day before the regular Sunday family visit. I had only a church medal to give Mom on her day, so I included a little note to express my feelings for her and tell her that she was the best mom ever. The hovering nun thought it was her duty to read it first and so intercepted the note just as I was giving it to Mom. I'll never forget the nun's reaction: "Your boy has a great gift and this letter is very beautiful. Not many mothers receive something like this." This was one of the rare moments of praise I received at school, and it has stayed with me.

I did not write anything again while I was in school, but the practice of retreating into my mind and my memories became a lifelong survival skill. Later, I began to write about my experiences as part of my healing. That process eventually led me to the writing of this book.

THE MÉNAGE

"Tee-adore!" The gruff voice of Sister S. shatters the silence of the study room. I cringe and slouch down at my desk—my fears are realized. I am nine years old and resident at the Fort Alexander Indian Residential School, 90 miles north of Winnipeg, Manitoba. The school is run by the Oblates, a religious order of the Roman Catholic Church, and is about two miles from my home on the Fort Alexander reserve.

C. has just returned and handed Sister S. a note with my name on it. I have an uncontrollable urge to yell and scream and disappear into nothingness. I do not have to respond to her calling my name. I know where I am expected to go.

Every evening before we go to bed, we are in our classrooms for study periods, and every night it happens. Four or five different boys are called into a room for a weekly ritual exercise known as *ménage*. We have learned that ménage is a French word for cleaning.

Can I escape? If I turn right instead of left when I leave the classroom, I can be outside without anyone seeing me for at least five minutes. Then I can stick to the ditches or the shoreline until I reach home. What then? Dad is probably working nightshift at the paper mill. Mom will be furious and threaten to take me right back, but then decide to wait for Dad to come home so that they can both take me back.

I decide I can't make it anyhow. Is anyone watching me? I can feel eyes on me, especially from the girls, who are segregated on the opposite side of the room in all our study sessions, as they are during regular classes. They know. It's my time for ménage—that weekly ritual, the washing of the genitals by a man in a black robe.

D. has a pained expression on his face as I catch his eye. He knows he's next or next or next. R. looks as if he enjoys my predicament. I feel the eyes on the other side of the room undressing me and imagining how I look, and what the little priest will do in a couple of minutes. That little *kookoosh* (pig). I feel a twang of guilt for thinking that, as he's the priest who baptized me.

A. almost has a look of pity on her face as she realizes that I will be bared, washed and dried and not one voice of protest will be heard. If there was, the promise of hell or purgatory would shut the protester up immediately if the slap on the back of the head or the pulling of the ear didn't.

I wait a few seconds, hoping the class will resume studying and doing their homework and forget about me. Sister S. peers above her glasses and I realize that if she calls my name again, everyone will refocus on my dilemma. Ugly witch! I'm sorry, God, I didn't mean that. But she is not pretty. If I go, the devil will not hang around me and give me bad thoughts, because clean crotches drive him away. He likes dirty crotches.

I wonder if they wash the girls, too. M. sitting over there looks clean enough, but S. must need washing every day! I should tell her that the next time she's mean to my little sister.

The horn-rimmed glasses turn my way again, so I'd better move. I close my book and fidget to find some way of marking my place. That will make Sister S. think I'm almost ready to go. There's R. looking at me again. I've seen him going to see Father more than once a week. I think he likes it. They should move him in with the priests or brothers. D. looks resigned, so I had better get it over with. It's probably been two or three seconds since my name was called. Someday I'll be away from here and everyone will forget what's happening to me at this very moment. I try to make as little noise as possible, and I crouch and attempt to become smaller as I struggle up from my desk.

I can feel my organ in the wrong place—it's supposed to be in my right pant leg, not my left! I wonder how many girls have noticed. I feel bowlegged because I've worn my jeans for a couple of weeks and the stiff canvas-like denim has sagged outward at the knees. It feels like my crotch is more prominently exposed. I feel nauseated, my muscles tighten, my jaw feels rigid, and I wonder if I can walk. There is something dreadfully wrong with my paraphernalia. I hope my fly is up. I hope my shorts don't ride up my arse, and I hope my shoes don't squeak. I also hope the girls don't know that in a couple of minutes I will have an erection.

As I slither along the aisle, I can feel 60 eyes on my back, my crimson face and my crotch. I don't turn around as I try to close the door softly behind me. I feel a breath of fresh air as I emerge from the classroom into the eerie, quiet, dimly lit hallway. I look left, down the long hall to my destination, and then turn right; I see the big doors that lead to the veranda and the fresh, crisp air and sparkling sky and fall breeze gently urging a soft, pillowy white cloud on its southerly journey. The geese and chickens must be abundant. The muskrats must be setting up for the winter. The deer must be fat. My dog must be wondering where I've gone.

The last time I ran away, Mom said I would have to answer to God for saying those things about Father P., and I got less of the fruit from Sister C. that Mom and Dad had brought me. I also didn't get to play hockey for five days. I think the priest is scared of Dad and that's why I didn't get the strap that time. He doesn't know that Dad would never harm anyone. Besides, I might tell Dad and he might believe that what Father P. does is not natural. My grandpa had a reputation in earlier encounters with priests when Dad and his siblings were first at the school. His protective nature regarding his family triggered very strong reactions.

I wish Dad were not so busy with his work and everything else. I think he'd like to take me out of school to teach me how to work, but he also wants me to learn and to finish school in order to get a better job.

I turn left, realizing I must go and finish this. It will be over soon.

As I slink down the hallway I hear coughing and shuffling of feet as I pass the classrooms with older boys and girls in them. I wonder why older boys don't have to go for ménage anymore. You must stay cleaner as you get older. I'll be in one of those classrooms soon, and I'll be one of the big boys. Then I can laugh and make fun of the younger boys when they go for their ménage.

Passing the chapel I think that I must go to confession tomorrow morning, because I couldn't take my eyes off Miss M.'s ankles the other day, and the outline of her legs on her dress. Miss M. is our teacher, and her dress hangs six inches off the floor. And that new sister—actually a novice, not quite a full-fledged nun and still without full nun regalia—has nice clean hands that felt warm and loving when she washed mine to clean a cut. My hands actually felt caressed and loved in the warm, soapy water.

I shuffle quietly down the hall. I think about the shop teacher, H., and wonder if he confesses to Father P. I wonder if he sinned when he pulled out his penis in front of me and commanded me to sit on the chair in front of him as he tried to pull it out by its roots. Maybe they're allowed. It looked like a big blood sausage, like the kind they make from a cow's blood when it's drained after slaughter.

In my mind, seeing Miss M.'s ankles, feeling good at the gentle touch of the novice nun and watching the shop teacher are all sins to be reported in the confessional. I wonder why there are so many questions from the confessional, and only from certain priests.

I wonder if the principal knows where I am going. The light casts a shadow on the door to his office; the door is closed again. I've heard that nuns go in there at night, probably to report on our bad behaviour during the day.

I see Father P.'s door and the light peeking out from under it. My imagination takes hold and I picture what I would do if in a split second I were to become a big man! I hesitate. Then, as my hand grasps the door handle, I catch an aroma of soap in a steamy, slimy soap holder. I wonder if the water will be warm.

• • •

There are many stories about Indian residential schools in Canada, stories about physical, sexual, spiritual and mental abuse. Some Church officials and other Canadians accuse Indian residential school survivors of "telling stories," implying that our stories are untrue or are exaggerated. The episode just described represents only a few minutes of my 12 years in the residential school system, but it is a scene etched in my memory. This ritual of "staying clean" happened every week or two over the years for many of the younger boys. It stopped when we became older and bigger, and our determination to threaten, maim, hurt or even kill our tormentors gave us the power to refuse the treatment.

My shop teacher, Mr. H., *was* a friendly and jovial guy who befriended young boys—in order to expose himself and talk dirty to them, I realize now. I recall that he forced me to unzip my trousers and expose myself to him, although I do not remember him touching me. But in exchanging stories with former classmates years later, I learned that he forced himself on other boys.

I do remember sitting, as a boy, with Mr. H. and his wife at the kitchen table in their residence, situated within the school grounds, with a bottle of beer, hating the taste but feeling excited as the beer slipped down my throat and warmed my belly. A survivor friend remembers drinking with Mr. H. and then having Mr. H. force him to lie on top of his wife as he stood aside and masturbated. I don't know if he ever made any other boys do that, but he certainly underwent a physical workout in front of me and others. This is one of the most belittling, embarrassing and hurtful memories I have had since then.

Recently such recollections have become more clear and part of my present reality. There are many like these, and they often come at awkward and unexpected moments. There are many gaps, but I am working to ensure that they become filled with missing memories, unpleasant as they may be. Each time I remember and talk about an experience, more and more comes back to me, helping me to see patterns of behaviour and understand the effects of my residential school experiences on my life.

My parents dropped me off at Fort Alexander Indian Residential School just days after I celebrated my seventh birthday, believing I would be cared for by the priests and nuns. Little did they know that the experience I was about to undergo for the next 12 years would shape and control my life for the next 40 or 50. From this point on, my life would not be my own. I would no longer be a son with a family structure. I would be parented by people who'd never known the joy of parenthood and in some cases hadn't been parented themselves.

The system was designed by the federal government to eliminate First Nations people from the face of our land and country, to rob the world of a people simply because our values and beliefs did not fit theirs. The system was racist and based on the assumption that we were not human but rather part animal, to be desavaged and moulded into something we could never become—white.

BROKEN CIRCLE

I am skipping along the old dirt road, the black, dry earth formed into ruts where horse-drawn wagons and rarely seen automobiles have gone by. I am on my way to a new adventure! I am going to be a "school kid." I'll learn to read; I'll be where my older brothers and sister were, where they learned new things, coming back smarter, bigger and ready to find jobs and make money like Dad, my uncles and our older cousins. I will be a school kid, and I'm excited!

Dad walks slightly ahead of Mom and me with a no-nonsense stride. He's like that. He's going to get where he's going, to see whoever he's going to see and get what he is getting, without wasting any time, whether by horse or on foot, with Blackie, Wolf, Bowser, Chico or one of his other constant canine sidekicks bounding along by his side.

Bright, colourful leaves flutter and fall gently onto the road and forest floor. There are formations of geese in the clear blue morning sky. Partridges and wild chickens are calling and thumping as they flirt and call for partners and mates. Their competition signals the beginning of fall. It is early September 1948, the beginning of the school year at Fort Alexander Indian Residential School.

This walk and its final destination will never leave my mind. The most vivid feeling I recall from that walk is my and Mom's playfulness. I often participate in workshops and conferences where facilitators get us to relieve stress by asking us to close our eyes and envision a relaxing scene, such as a favourite place when we were young. Mine has always been this scene of me skipping and scrambling along the peaceful road, birds singing and a dog—mine, probably—barking occasionally.

Nothing else mattered as I played a sort of tag with Mom, pretending she couldn't catch me and then settling in beside Dad to walk with him for a while before starting the game again. My enthusiasm would be momentarily damped when I tripped on a crack or rut in the road. Mom would ignore my whimpering at first, as she and Dad kept up their pace. Then she'd turn and walk backward, making a face at me and trying to wrinkle her mouth so as to make it look like a guitar. In our household, this was a way of teasing me to deflect any "babyness"—my older brothers and sisters called me "guitar mouth" whenever I tried to get pity and support by whimpering and crying. Mom's actions always brought me back to reality and made me think my hurt was non-existent or minor, and my tears make-believe. The scenario always ended with tears mixing with laughter.

I was the youngest boy in our family but the first of a second batch of children for Mom and Dad. My older siblings, Cliff, Leon and Marie, were all born within five years of each other. I came along eight years later, followed by three more girls. The older kids spoiled me, as did Mom and Dad, and from family stories and anecdotes it seems they had fun watching me grow up. I think they occasionally inflicted a little discomfort on me so that they could enjoy my "guitar mouth." But they all grew up to be kind and gentle individuals, and I smile to myself when I remember the delight and fun they had at my expense.

Often in residential school, and even as an adult, I would stand before a mirror and pucker my lips to see whether indeed my mouth could look like a guitar. Periodically I still try to recreate that look, but I can't get away from the notion that my lips are too small to form a shape resembling a guitar.

Although my older siblings must have endured and remembered the sadness of residential school, and the trauma of separation, those times we spent together at home as Mom and Dad's children bring me memories and moments of great joy.

Walking with Mom and Dad on that life-changing day in September 1948, I remember no confusion, no sadness, no desperation, only joy and innocence on a trek that seems now to have taken longer than it actually did. I'd walked this road many times with Dad and Grandpa Schall on our way to hunt and to check snares and traps along the river and close to the road. The old Hudson's Bay Company store, established on the shore of the Winnipeg River in the 1700s, was about a mile west of our home. In 1948, there were no other houses between our place and the store, and there were only four houses between the store and the residential school, about another mile farther to the west. The narrow road was protected on both sides by a thick growth of trees and brush. The road has since become one of the busiest highways in the area, and much forest and land have been lost due to the seven hydroelectric dams on the beautiful Winnipeg River.

But on this day, it was quiet except for my and Mom's laughter and yelling. Squirrels chattered at us and birds screeched disapproval at our intrusion. During a lull on our journey, we talked of residential school and my questions about it. A dominant memory that comes to me about that hour is Mom's reassurance and excitement about my learning to read.

I'd watched my brothers read Dell and Marvel comic books and been intrigued by their intense focus on the bubbles above characters' heads. Sometimes they'd paraphrase the story in Ojibway for me, as all I could say and understand in English then was "hello," "good day, eh?," "yes, please" and "no, please." (Mom had taught me that "please" was one of the most important words in the white man's language. I recall refusing a glass of milk from one of Mom's "white ladies," because I was shy, with a "no, please." The white ladies were the women in town who employed Mom to do their housework.) My brothers' translations were very exciting and brought a whole new world to my little "Indian" life. They instilled in me a strong desire to read these comic books for myself. I didn't want anything to do with those other books that my sister read, which had to do with girls and boys looking into each other's eyes, hugging each other and, as my sister said, falling in love. Only mothers were allowed to hug their kids that closely.

So Mom would say, in Ojibway, "When you go to school, you will be able to read comics." In my mind, this would be the greatest benefit of my schooling, and Mom and even Dad used this to fuel my desire whenever the subject of school came up. The first and probably only positive reason why I should go to residential school was now deeply entrenched in my young mind. And so at four, five and six years of age I had set my first goal, other than delivering a deer, partridge or rabbit to the kitchen table.

Mom had high hopes that I would go on to be successful in something away from the reserve. Her goal was for us to be just as good as the white kids and do what they could do. Mom was a God-fearing Christian who was easily and deeply influenced by the Church, particularly by the sermons of the priests at the church and the school. Her mother died when Mom was very young, and her dad, Niizhotaens, had let her be taken away by the nuns. (His name means "Little Niizhotay," as his father was named Niizhotay. The priests convinced him to be baptized with the English name Duncan Twoheart.)

Thus the nuns and priests of the school had become her parents. They had no knowledge about our culture and could not provide traditional parenting. Mom lived at the school until the summer she turned 17, and then she married Dad. Luckily, her mother-in-law, my granny, mentored all her daughters-in-law on how to be effective wives and mothers. I don't know anything else about Mom's life up to that point, and she never talked to any of us about her experiences. I shudder to think how she was brought up, but her story can never surface now, at least not in this world.

There had been no choice for Mom. The uncertainty and fears she felt for me, her little boy, were overcome by her dreams that I would learn to talk "good English" and find a steady job that would take me away somewhere and let me enjoy fineries and extra joys such as indoor toilets, electric lights and heat on cold winter nights. She hoped that all the amenities white people enjoyed would someday be mine.

It is strange that I can recall the journey to the school but not our actual leaving home or reaching the school. In my memory I am suddenly alone in the entrance parlour of the school, sitting on a bench and trying to hear the conversation in the office. After a moment, Mom and Dad emerged from the office, followed by a priest in a scary black robe. He looked very big and serious and agitated. Perhaps his white collar was uncomfortable, I thought— too tight. His slightly scuffed black shoes poked out from under his robe, reminding me of the demonic characters in the stories told by Mom and my aunts of visitors who danced with party-goers on Saturday nights.

In these stories, handsome strangers appeared just before midnight at dances and parties, well-dressed, jovial and friends to all. They danced flamboyantly and skilfully with the ladies. As they whirled past the people taking a break, lamps and candles would begin to flicker, and the resting dancers would be horrified to see that the shiny black shoes had turned into hooves and that smooth, pointy tails were flicking out from under the men's coattails as couples sailed by. Then the lamps and candles would die out briefly, and when they reignited, the strangers would be gone. They'd depart the same way they had arrived: in an elaborate black-silk-covered buggy pulled by two powerful jet-black stallions, their neck collars adorned with decorative little bells on chains. All would be quiet on the dance floor as the partygoers listened to the hooves and the clinking of the horses' chains fading into the distance as the horses delivered their masters to another dance. Then it would be Sunday morning, a holy day; the unholy visit had been a warning.

It was strange to have these thoughts come to me as I looked at this big, black-robed man in the parlour, knowing as I did how Mom, Dad and the whole community heeded the priests and nuns and their Church teachings about the constant presence of the devil and evil. My parents lived with the fear and belief that if we didn't listen and practise what we were taught by the Church, we would be lost forever and suffer eternal damnation in the fires of hell.

This big, black-robed man in the parlour was made even scarier and more bewildering to me by the enormous crucifix stuck into the black satin-like sash around his belly. The sash resembled the traditional Métis sash worn at ceremonies and celebrations. As my eyes darted to his feet, I felt some relief that poking out from under his robe were still just two scruffy shoes. The crucifix in the sash later reminded me of Roy Rogers, Randolph Scott and other cowboys we saw each Friday night in the cowboy movies, their guns sticking out of holsters hanging from their hips. I don't remember the names of the bad guys in those movies, but this scary man could have been one of the gunslingers dressed in black with a 10-gallon hat on his head.

My previous encounters with priests and nuns had been non-threatening, as I had had some control over them. I can remember watching my sister Marie leave the church after Sunday Mass when she was still in school and I was perhaps four or five. As was the custom, community members stood around outside and visited after church. The priests and sometimes the nuns also came out and mingled. Only after everyone else had left the church did the residential school kids come out to march in double file back to the school, not once being allowed to chat and visit with their families. So went Marie and presumably my brother Leon. My oldest brother, Cliff, being in his late teens, would already have left school. I remember the sadness on Marie's face, although Mom and Dad would have an opportunity to visit her at school for a little while that afternoon.

It was here outside the church that parents and children, siblings and friends, aunts and uncles, cousins and neighbours had a chance to glance at each other and acknowledge each other with a look, a smile, a little wave and perhaps a whispered "*ahneen* (hello)." I wondered why my sister couldn't come home with us and share in our Sunday meal, as she did during summer holidays.

Priests and nuns didn't make me apprehensive then: I'd been in open spaces and could run around without feeling trapped by rooms and the closeness of black-robed strangers. I could scamper away if and when they came over to where Dad or uncles and friends were visiting. I had the option of running to where Mom was, as the priests, brothers and other male staff only forced themselves on the circles of men.

I couldn't comprehend the nature of their teachings, the way they instilled fear and apprehension in my parents and the rest of the congregation. I still don't understand the power those teachings had; I can only assume that the spirituality of our people invoked a strong and deep respect and fear for the messenger and his helpers. The priest was the messenger and representative of the Creator they called God.

So this encounter in the entrance parlour was completely new to me, and for the first time in my life I felt trapped. Mom came over and sat beside me. She wrapped her hand around mine, and I felt desperation growing in me. I looked over at Dad, who had his back toward us and was staring out the screened parlour door, the ever-present hat in his hands. He was obviously concerned by what I was going through and wanted no part of my discomfort and crying, as if to say he wasn't the cause of it. He was letting Mom take care of it.

I started to whimper, not understanding why but sensing that something awful was about to happen to me. Mom consoled me and held on tightly to my hand. Hers felt warm, protective and soft in spite of the roughness caused by years of constant hard work. Her glance was gentle and loving, and her lovely brown eyes were beginning to tear.

Suddenly a door opened, and two older cousins of mine, Marcel and Clem, entered the parlour. They glanced cautiously at the priest, then stood there as Mom rose and gave each of them one of my hands. I started bawling and struggled to break free of their grasp as Mom kissed me on the forehead and told my cousins, in Ojibway, to look after me. I understood clearly then that she was leaving me. I was scared. It was worse than my fear of seeing the doctor when I was sick, for those times I knew Mom would always be there waiting for me.

The priest said something inaudible in English and Dad responded somehow. He and Mom quickly went out the door, down the stairs and onto the road that led home. I was left alone and confused, wondering why they would leave me there.

Thus were born the abandonment issues I would struggle with for years henceforth. There was no plausible explanation for my being locked up and not being able to be with my family. My trust in my parents was shattered. It would take me years to understand that trust goes hand in hand with understanding why a loved one does things. Sometimes broken trust never heals.

Over 50 years later as I write these recollections, I feel a huge lump in my throat as I think of Mom and imagine how she felt. I can't hold back my tears as I realize her heart must have been breaking at having to let me go. I weep and sob. Waves of anger, hurt, love, tenderness and desperation accompany this vision of Mom's kind and loving face. I deeply regret not having spent more time with her, to hug her and tell her I loved her, to treasure her.

I feel suddenly panicky and need desperately to talk to my wife. I telephone and she answers. I can hardly talk, but she knows something is wrong. She waits to hear what part of my story has affected me today. I've found my rock; she brings me back to safety, back to reality. I'm not fighting this alone. This thing, this residential school syndrome, is cruel and won't go away. I must, and will, live through it. I wasn't alone, and we can as survivors take something positive from our experience. I remind myself that somewhere, sometime, someone has and is enduring something worse.

• • •

I don't recall anything else from that moment other than feelings of panic, desperation, anger and hopelessness. My chest was pounding, and I tried to catch my breath and loosen my cousins' hold as they led me through the door and into the hall, into the place that would be my home for the next 10 years.

I thought how the grips on my runners would have made it easier to stop my cousins from taking me into that unknown. But I had on the ugly black Oxfords Mom had made me wear. One part of her indoctrination into the ways of the white ladies she cleaned house for was proper dress. Bare feet or stinky, worn-out runners weren't proper attire for occasions like this.

I twisted and turned, kicked and yelled, and even tried to bite as I was practically dragged down the hall. Not once was there any intervention by the priest, who had quickly disappeared into his office. The significance of that hit me years later when I realized that the arrival and prominence of my cousins in this time of discomfort and terror was intended to shift the pain, hurt and blame toward them and, more particularly, Mom and Dad.

I had felt an overwhelming anger toward my parents as they walked away. I could not imagine what they'd talk about heading home, but knew it would be mostly a walk of silence. Dad would be his usual self and not say much. Mom would be quieter than usual. They'd force themselves to talk about small things, just to overcome their sense of having betrayed their youngest boy. There would be a touch of anger and guilt, regret and helplessness.

I learned years later, in a session with a therapist, that this abandonment not only had a huge effect on my personality and how I'd lived to that point, but also gave rise to a reaction in me—guilt and guilt transfer—that had affected everyone I knew, particularly people I love. I think all residential school survivors suffer from this; in fact, anyone who has experienced long-term abandonment may develop this characteristic. You feel guilt for the most insignificant things, even when it doesn't make the slightest sense. Almost always that guilt becomes blame, and when it's turned inward, you feel you've done something wrong. My first reaction to most situations is to become defensive and aggressive as I think: "What did I do wrong?"

Sometimes I blame others and so transfer the guilt to those I love most. For example, once during summer holidays, when we were expected to handle chores around the house, I told my younger sister Marge that we'd probably not be able to visit our aunt and cousins because Mom thought I wasn't well enough to go. I had sprained my shoulder from hauling so many pails of water up the riverbank by myself. I told Marge that if she'd helped me with my chore, perhaps I'd not have injured myself and we could have played with our cousins. The guilt I laid on her must have been overwhelming; she was two years younger than me and looked up to me as her older brother who could do no wrong.

At residential school, and in my life afterwards, I continued to pull guilt trips on my family and friends. My attitude was

I drew this picture as an adult, after I'd begun my healing journey. It depicts my being left at residential school a few days after my seventh birthday.

reinforced and further strengthened by my hatred of being locked up at residential school, and by the behaviour of the nuns and priests themselves. I remember a nun telling my cousin that her baby brother had died because she'd been bad. My cousin was not yet 10 years old at the time; she believed that the death was her fault. I can only imagine her reaction to other bad situations throughout her life as a result of this experience.

My parents weren't exempt from my blaming. I recall a post-Mass visit on a particular Sunday when Mom and Dad had been delayed at church and were a little late coming to the visiting area. Students were only called to this area when their parents had arrived, so I'd been one of the students kept away from there. Then, for some unknown reason, I was only called over 15 or 20 minutes after Mom and Dad had arrived. Although I knew that Mom would never miss an opportunity to visit, I was perturbed that they had left me to wonder if they were coming. My anger was silent but obvious, and it hurt them, especially Mom. After that, if Mom was even a few minutes late arriving, she made sure to explain what had happened to cause the delay.

As a child, I didn't understand the guilt that Mom and Dad experienced by leaving me at school—guilt that was compounded every week when they visited and then had to leave me again. I would transfer guilt to them over trivial things like the type or amount of fruit that Mom brought me each week.

Always wondering what I'd done wrong, I had to push my guilt and self-blame onto them. They had to live with this pain.

Dad would have dealt with this pain by keeping busy with work at the mill and with trapping, hunting, gathering and helping others on the reserve. That would have been his refuge from the guilt of leaving his son behind. Mom would have carried the burden with her belief that I'd finish school and be the first in our family to "graduate." This was a word she'd learned from the white ladies, who bragged about their children either having graduated and now having great jobs and great lives or being about to graduate and get the kinds of jobs that Mom often hadn't even heard of.

I don't remember anything else about the moment I was handed over to my cousins and can only imagine the difficulty they had trying to calm me down and settle me into the boys' playroom. This was where we spent our time when we weren't in class, in the dormitory, at church or in the school chapel, or playing and working outside. It was really no different from the common area in places like penitentiaries and provincial jails.

I do vividly remember lying on a bed, probably on my first day, with rows of beds behind and beside me with other boys in them. I was confused and hurt, and trying to see whether the windows provided an escape route. The doors were closed, and they were right beside a room where the nun, or "sister," as we knew her, occasionally peeked at us through her curtained window.

Because of my whimpering and other boys' crying, the nun emerged that first night several times to walk around the dormitory. As she passed, it would be quiet for a while. She'd stop briefly to whisper something to console the young children in various beds. Although my English was then very limited, her words and manner were somewhat soothing when she whispered to me. The soft pat of her fingers as she ran them through my hair provided some calm. I was scared of this woman in black, but she appeared to understand my pain and sorrow, and I thought she might hold me until I fell asleep. I remember thinking she must be a kind mother to someone and that she might be like a mother to me until I could go home. I didn't know that nuns couldn't be mothers.

The older boys were stronger and more able to handle the separation from their parents. My adjustment to school life and my relationship to white culture were just beginning. I like to think that the kindness shown by this black-robed woman was genuine and not merely a way to gain my trust. It did instill in me a spark of trust that lessened the pain of capture.

I was fortunate that first night that this sister was one of the kind ones. My experience over the next few years would prove that not all were kind and loving. But that night, the nun's fingers on my head and in my hair provided some reassurance, and I eventually cried myself to sleep.

THE MORNING ROUTINE

Most mornings at school I awakened with quite a hunger, as did most of my schoolmates, and I wished for Mom's steaming bannock, which she made in the early morning, coming out of the oven. I remembered vividly her flitting about in her patterned apron with her red plaid tea towel and oven mitt. She'd lean the steaming bannock against the stove, massage it with oil and lard spread on wax paper to soften the brown crust, dust it lightly with flour and then let it sit for a few moments so that it would retain its texture. The aroma was unbelievable, and as I lay awake in the early hours at residential school I wondered if I would ever experience again the comfort and satisfaction of being with Mom at the start of the day.

Before anyone else was up, and even before the morning sun peeked in, Dad would be bustling about, tinkering with the firewood to prepare wood chips for his buck stove. Before long the hiss and crackle of pine and tamarack logs would fill the cool morning air. Soon Mom would appear, warming her body against the stove as it heated up.

I would lie under my feather robe, waiting for the warm air to drift in from the kitchen and for Mom to be well into her routine by the stove before joining her. Every morning she asked the same question, in Ojibway of course: "Why are you up? Go back to bed!" Knowing she actually enjoyed my company, I'd sit by the stove and get toasty warm, and she would engulf me in one of her multicoloured, patchwork blankets. I still have one of them, not from that early era, but from later years.

Dad worked for 30 years at the paper mill in town and Mom worked for just as long in the homes of some of the managers and workers from the mill. She was also busy at home, running our household, washing and cleaning, shopping, cooking, sewing, gardening, helping extended family and spending time with and learning from Grandma Therese. She was even a member of the church choir. We took her for granted then and now wonder how she did it all.

Those early mornings when I joined her, I delighted in watching her prepare food for the day and for Dad's lunch. Any breaks from making stews and soups, baking or waiting for the bannock to be ready were not wasted. She'd sit by me in her woollen nightgown and moccasins, mending socks, gloves and other clothing.

She talked to me then about things I didn't always understand, but I vaguely remember them as stories about her own family. Mom was a good storyteller, and her stories of family life and values hastened the rising sun. I know Dad also enjoyed these moments. I'd catch him hovering close by to hear parts of Mom's stories. He'd call her the *att soo kay quay* (storyteller woman). Through this early-morning togetherness I began to know her family, not fully realizing that it was mine, too. If only I'd known then that it would be impossible to relive these moments after I'd gone to school. Perhaps I'd have paid more attention if I had understood that these history lessons were unique and that only my mom could relate them. I wish I'd retained more of what she told me. I didn't learn most of this family history because of being isolated at residential school.

Mom's first batch of bannock usually consisted of two golden-brown masterpieces that each measured probably about 18 inches across. She'd dust them with flour after they'd cooled for a few minutes, then slice one in half, and a slight cloud of flour would puff up into the air. Then I was on my way, cutting my own slices. Lard or butter would ooze through the fine texture and create a rising steam that had an indescribably delicious aroma. Mom's homemade jam mingled with the butter or lard to create a heavenly pre-breakfast snack.

Some mornings my younger sister Marge emerged from her hammock, dragging her loose diaper. I would tuck her on my lap under the blanket or feather robe that Mom had wrapped around me. Marge was three years younger than I was, and I was her big, protective brother.

I'm thankful that this sweet memory of Mom and me has stayed with me. Even now, early morning is my time to savour the thought of Mom and the conversations she had with me, her little boy, in the kitchen.

When my tummy remembered those moments as I lay on my cot at residential school, I would wonder again why I was there. I'd wonder why I couldn't have stayed at home, and why my older sister Marie couldn't have lived with us instead of at school. Thoughts of home brought on tears.

It is somewhat fortunate that we didn't have much time at residential school to feel sorry for ourselves lying in bed early in the morning, or much time to daydream. Morning Mass in the school chapel was at seven, and the chore of getting ready for it was very regimented. First, we had to get up and kneel by our beds and say the morning prayer, led by the supervisor. In my early years, that was usually a nun. Later, when I was one of the big boys, it was usually a brother, a man also dressed in a black robe; I don't recall now whether brothers wore the big crucifix across their stomachs.

What I do remember about some of those brothers was their sharp-pointed shoes that made me not want to sit. When they thought you were too slow or not listening, you'd get a swift kick.

You became very quick and learned to twist your arse so as not to get the brunt of the kick between the cheeks. I became very adept at that little trick. But, oh, the pain if for some reason you didn't expect the boot or weren't quick enough to turn the other cheek.

When we'd finished morning prayer, we were required to pull back our blankets to the foot of the bed, to expose the sheet. A nun then walked around and inspected each bed. There were probably 40 to 50 beds, in rows of 8 to 10. Once in a while she'd stop and order the boy whose bed she'd just inspected to strip off the sheet and take it to the front of the dorm, beside the sinks, and put the sheet over his head. Sometimes you could see stains on the sheet. Sometimes there was just a trace, almost too small to see, yet somehow the nun, on close inspection, would see that spot of yellow.

This wasn't a daily occurrence; accidents happened perhaps once a week, but the sheet-wearers were almost always the same boys. They had to stand there at the front of the dorm until the rest of us had gone to the bathroom, washed our faces and hands, brushed our teeth with a white chalky powder and returned to make our beds. Many times I heard the whimpering and quiet sobs of the boy under the sheet. Sometimes he suffered further pain from older, meaner boys who called him *shee sheeg i cheet* (pissy arse), *ween jeegi pinjik* (stinky crotch), *ween jee gis* (stinky) and other descriptive names in Ojibway. (My translations are purely phonetic, as I don't know how to write in Ojibway.)

Many mornings I awakened early with horror at feeling my crotch, fingering my underwear and finding an imagined dampness. The slightest indication of wetness on my sheets would mean standing in front of my friends and cousins for all to see what I'd done. Luckily, I always managed to awaken when the need to pee arose! I always felt sorry for the boys who slept too soundly to feel the urge coming on. I remember me and other neighbours of bedwetters whispering at night in an effort to wake them and get them up to go to the bathroom. I used to think the bedwetters were at fault. I now realize that there are many causes for bedwetting, emotional and physical, and that we process different things in different ways.

I used to think also that our "protectors and guardians" were insufficiently trained and incapable of helping. I now believe their actions were an indication that they lacked parenting skills, as they never demonstrated any ability in helping and counselling the boys. In fact, I detected cruel satisfaction in some of these supervisors and now realize that they were simply mean.

Perhaps some of them never learned what should have been taught to them by their own parents. Some priests and nuns had escaped strict, unreasonable and malfunctioning families by entering religious orders. Their biases and unreasonable reactions to children must have been, in part, a result of their own upbringing. They had learned well how to order, dictate to and use superior force to run the schools.

Getting ready for early Mass always involved lineups. We got in line to do our morning business, with the occasional accident in the lineup. You had to learn the art of fidgeting to curtail the urgings of nature, because you couldn't leave your spot in line. The consequences of the accidents that happened periodically in the lineup could be as bad as those endured by bedwetters. Then we got in line to wash our faces and brush our hair. We finally got in line to go to the chapel.

Generally, morning Mass had no special significance other than it was one of the rare occasions when the girls were near the boys. Brothers and sisters had a chance to be close and even brush against each other as they returned from going up to receive Communion.

In my first couple of years, we boys sat on one side of the chapel and the girls sat on the other. Because the aisle between us was only three or four feet wide, we were almost sitting beside girls our own age. In those years, in my innocence, I didn't feel sorry for the bigger boys and girls sitting, kneeling and standing in such close proximity; I didn't know yet what they might have been going through as adolescence and puberty crept into their lives. Boys had girlfriends, girls had boyfriends, even at residential school, but they had very little opportunity to talk and interact, let alone hold hands. Nevertheless, hormones have no mercy and do not discriminate. I later heard that saltpetre was used to enhance the taste of some of our food, particularly porridge, and that it subdued raging hormones.

I was lucky not to experience this plight. By the time I was that age, the supervisors had changed the format and the boys sat in the back rows, behind the girls. That meant that the littlest guys in the first couple of rows sat behind the older girls, with one empty row separating them. This row was occupied only by a big, grouchy, scary nun, whose occasional glances at the littlest boys directly behind her had a decided quieting effect. The new format also meant that I never saw what was happening at the front of the chapel and could not make eye contact with my own sister or smile at girls my own age. This tactic for preventing contact between hormone-driven young people was mostly effective, except when Communion was offered. Then almost all the boys would make their way to the front to receive the sacrament, passing close by to the girls, even when they hadn't had time to go to confession beforehand because of "big sins."

I had difficulty differentiating between venial and mortal (big) sins, so I received Communion many times without confession. Confession became a secondary consideration for older boys, who celebrated Communion to be close to the girls and not because if they didn't the nuns and priests would know they had big sins.

The stares from the nuns and other supervisors attending Mass if you had *not* gone to Communion were agonizing. You resolved to do all you could to be first in line at the next Friday's confessional. I remember as a young boy keeping my eyes glued to the floor if I hadn't gone up for the sacrament, sure that the priests and nuns would know I had committed some act they saw as a sin. It was difficult to keep track of your sins, especially during complex and probing questioning by Father P. at ménage time. If you had stared at the ankles of one of the pretty nuns, not even knowing why, then you wondered if that was a sin because Father P. asked whether you had stared. Sometimes I found myself blushing for no reason under the stare of a nun or brother.

After morning Mass, we filed out in a line to go to our respective common playrooms, where we were corralled until breakfast. Here we used the toilets and were required again to wash up before lining up to go to the refectory to eat.

Once a week, boys and girls were assigned chores. Every morning, at noon and before supper, two or three boys were to ensure that the furnaces were loaded with wood. Another trio made sure that incoming wood was piled appropriately in the furnace rooms. Girls helped in the kitchen with cleaning and putting away utensils. Other chores were cleaning, sweeping or washing toilets.

Those of us not assigned chores were herded outdoors to play. The boys' playground had a baseball field, swings and an outdoor skating rink in winter. After school and after meals we'd be sent out on this open field. The weather had to be extreme for us to stay indoors. Most days were sunny and bright, as was normal in Manitoba. Pouring rain found us crowded into the playroom, as did blizzards and -40°F temperatures. Those were the only times when we weren't sent outside, even if someone was not well. I remember shivering students huddled close to a building, eyes watering and snot running down their noses, trying to escape the blowing snow or rain that normally wouldn't bother them. Sometimes it was me huddled there.

The assigned tasks remained pretty well the same; only the workers changed each week. If you were one of the sweepers or cleaners, you prayed for weather that allowed outside activities before classes began. Chores were made more difficult and took longer when mischievous students ran across the dust-laden floors, occupied toilets, splashed water and generally got in the way. The absence of kids allowed you to finish your chores early and spend what little time you had left enjoying the outdoors before lining up for classes.

The first half of the morning was spent with three or four grades in one classroom, reading, writing and doing arithmetic. After recess, which allowed us to use up some energy, we went back to the classroom for the last hour and a half before lunch to learn about religion and the catechism from a priest. The no-nonsense attitude of Father C. was sometimes scary, and you had to be on your best behaviour and look studious and religious. Before his sessions, you also had to be sure you had taken good care of your bathroom needs and duties. You lived precariously if your tummy was upset.

The first time I ran away from school was due to my encountering this exact predicament. Grades 4 and 5 had been in class for over an hour with Father C. and his catechism lesson. About half an hour before lunch, I raised my arm to signal that I had to go to the toilet. I had begun to wiggle because I needed to have a bowel movement. My persistence finally elicited an angry response from Father C.: he flung a blackboard eraser at me and shouted that I could wait. I succumbed and shat, very quietly, into my pants.

Two or three neighbouring classmates knew what I had done but remained quiet. When it was time to leave at noon, Father C. stood outside the classroom as the other students filed out row by row. I stayed behind, leaning against the blackboard. I waited until all was quiet and then slipped away through the back door of the veranda. As it was early winter, my excrement had frozen to my rear by the time I arrived home, much to Mom's chagrin. She cleaned me up and fed me some soup. It was wonderful to be home. My joy at being there was short-lived, however, as Dad eventually returned from his afternoon shift at the mill.

Although he seemed in no hurry to take me back to school, Mom insisted that I return immediately because the nuns and the principal, Father C., would be unhappy. That evening I was back in the entrance parlour at the school. After my parents had left, my forearms met the priest's strap and I was told I couldn't accompany our hockey team into town for our next game. The news of my dilemma had reached my classroom by then, and I could tell that some boys were delighted by what had happened to me. I was embarrassed.

Except for early-fall and other seasonal duties, our morning and after-lunch activities were routine. Anticipation of Sunday parental visits was always at the forefront of our minds. Activities out of the norm hastened the time between visits, so deviations from routine were almost occasions for jubilation. We looked forward to major activities such as picking potatoes and vegetables for parts of each day for two or three weeks at a time. Building and dismantling skating rinks, repairing structures and cleaning barns became welcome activities. Because the chores and jobs took us away from the confines of the school and the classroom, we took on the challenges with enthusiasm and prolonged their completion as much as we could.

I find it very perplexing and sad to realize now that my life at the school during those years didn't contribute anything that helped or prepared me for the outside world. We lived with a routine based on fear, caution, shame, guilt and an overwhelming need to appear to be good and to obey the rules and wishes of the nuns and priests.

FAMILY GATHERINGS
AT THE POINT

I remember and treasure times of feeling happy, protected and safe from when I was at home as a young boy and from even later in life with Mom and the family. One of my most vivid memories is of Mom, my sister Marie, Aunt Irene, her daughter Ikwense ("little woman") and sometimes other aunts and their children going to the point of land stretching from our house to the Winnipeg River. This point, mostly granite, was almost like an island, with growths of small oak, aspen, chokecherry and other small trees and bushes, and it reached a few hundred feet out into the water. It was one of many small peninsulas that jutted out into the river and provided ideal locations for family activities for those lucky enough to live near them.

Over the years, outcroppings of these huge deposits of pre-Cambrian granite had created bays within the river system that became havens for recreation, boat-landing, swimming and fish-cleaning. Our point had been used for years as a look-out, as you could see for some distance toward Pine Falls to the southeast, and as a stopping-off place for canoe travellers coming from eastern Canada and from the north, from Churchill, the Hudson Bay area and the Arctic Ocean. Explorers, hunters and traders going past our land on the river often stopped for food, rest and friendship on these shores and points.

Our mothers, grannies and big sisters spent one or two days a week by the water at these points washing clothes on flat sections of rock. Those days would be used for that purpose only. They were festive occasions and nothing else was done around the house. Young children's naps and meals and older children's playtimes all happened there. Only occasional trips to the house were taken, to fetch more soap, food or drinks. The excitement was overwhelming for us kids.

I remember my cousin Dee-ainse ("small Dee") and I spending five to six hours a day in the water. I didn't know his real name was Howard until years later, and I have no idea how he came to be called Dee. He was adventurous and industrious, and even though he was only a year or two older than me, he taught me many things. He had gone to residential school for one year before I was sent there. Then his dad, Old Joe Gus (there was a younger Joe Gus, too, on the reserve), pulled him from school to help the family.

In those early years, the churches and the government would allow some families to keep their children at home. If it could be demonstrated that a family was unable to manage their household without the child, then that child was allowed to live at home to help his aging or unwell parents and grandparents. I knew few children in this category. And I envied the ones I did know who were lucky enough to be day students.

Old Joe had gone to the industrial residential school in St. Boniface, although it was more than a day's trek from Fort Alexander as the eagle flies and through bush around Lake Winnipeg to the Red River and eventually St. Boniface. He was sent there to study carpentry and religion. He never formally taught Dee the fine art of carpentry, but Dee was a free spirit, easily taking on activities like building, trapping, fishing, forestry, hunting and other survival skills and endeavours. He could teach himself how to do anything. For example, he learned to swim just by watching and then swimming with my brother Cliff.

Cliff was an incredible swimmer of great distances. He was known on the reserve and even in neighbouring towns as one of the best swimmers in the area. He would swim across the river and back, and even down to the mission by the residential school, which was one and a half to two miles away, trying to beat his best time. He thought Dee was a great swimmer for a little guy. "*Cap shkoo keego*," he'd say, "like a fish." Such praise from his older cousin, a locally renowned swimmer and near celebrity, heightened Dee's efforts, and he'd try to duplicate Cliff's achievements, bringing me along, of course.

While mothers and sisters did the wash, it was a fun time for the young boys and girls to frolic and play. Although families worked hard washing, scrubbing, wringing out and hanging up family bedding and clothing, and patching items in disrepair, there was also fun and festivity, and the air was filled with the sounds of people swimming, chasing each other, laughing and teasing one another.

Our mothers and sisters kept a fire going all day. They slowed down just long enough to plop down on the handmade quilts and feather robes and enjoy a huge picnic of fresh bannock cooked in a frying pan over the fire, fried deer or moose meat, and weiners plucked directly from the pan and put into waiting bannock. Our meals were topped off by desserts, usually store-bought cookies and doughnuts, and Kool-Aid or sweetened tea. Baked goodies seemed to be a staple in our home and something sweet always emerged from Dad's lunch bucket (with my help) when he returned from work.

I still enjoy visiting that place, although erosion along the river has altered the site. In the early 1990s, erosion near the point revealed the burial site of one of my ancestors. The remains have since been relocated—illegally it seems—to another site somewhere within the reserve and not at the cemetery. The decision to relocate our relative's remains, and how it was to be done, was made through the Province of Manitoba's archaeological authority, the Fort Alexander chief and council, and an elder from the north-central area of the United States. Our families, some of whom still reside at this point of land, could easily have been consulted about the new burial site, but never were. Research is underway to repatriate the missing remains. The discovery of the skeletal remains on family land awakened strong emotions in my late Uncle Albert. In reminiscing about his youth, he indicated that this grave wasn't the only one at the point and that eventually other lost ancestors would be discovered. He talked about that whole point of land with reverence and hoped it wouldn't be disturbed.

The little bay between our point and what we called Treaty Point has always been a gathering place for my family, including our neighbouring cousins and other extended family, since before Treaty 1 in 1871 and the laying out of our reserve in 1876. Before the treaty, this piece of land was owned and cleared by my great-grandfather—my grandma Therese's father, Jean-Baptiste (J.B.) Charbonneau. He left the land to her. He and his family had settled adjacent to where Moise Fontaine, my grandpa Charles' father, was situated. So those two great-grandfathers had cleared and worked the land for years before it became part of the Fort Alexander reserve. It was then passed on to Uncle Albert by his mother, Therese, as he was the youngest boy in the family.

The two families joined forces when my grandparents, Charles (Schall) Fontaine, born in 1865, and Therese Charbonneau, born in 1873, were married in 1893. I am still awestruck at times that I actually knew, listened and talked to people from the 1800s. Time passes quickly. The attitudes and feelings of invincibility, and the belief that "I will do it later" or "I will have time later," are almost gone as I battle chronic back pain, uncooperative knees and a memory that has lost most of the teachings and history given to me by my parents and grandparents. Soon I will be in a very small minority of people who've known and talked to someone who lived before 1900. But at least the strong family relationships created by my ancestors and ingrained in their descendants have left me with a deep sense of love, closeness and oneness with my own family.

I was born on September 7, 1941, at the Pine Falls Indian Hospital. It wasn't really an Indian hospital but merely part of the Pine Falls Hospital, which took care of Indians from the Fort Alexander, Hole River (Hollow Water) and Black River reserves. The facility also provided care and treatment for residents of Bad Throat, which is known today by its original name, Manigotagan. It's a community that began as an Indian village before the signing of Treaty 1. Although it's mostly Métis, the church, police and white townspeople made no distinction between Métis and Indians.

The nicest part of the hospital was reserved for the whites of Pine Falls and for non-Indians from surrounding areas. Indian employees at the mill were given priority over other Indians for treatment and beds. As Dad was a long-time steady employee, Mom knew about the preferential treatment and was proud that we were part of the "elite" from the reserve because it meant recognition and better treatment for her family in all aspects of life around Pine Falls.

Mom was a very humble, generous, kind person, and the pride she felt was because her children and family got special concessions and favours by having "succeeded" in the outside world and were thus served and treated much like her white ladies and their families. It wasn't selfish pride, but rather satisfaction that her children and husband got some recognition and honour. Later, when I was 15 and 16, I was hired at the mill for two summers when Dad, who was highly regarded there, convinced the foreman that I was a good worker, and I got to be known as "the man who worked at the mill."

Mom's pride was perhaps her strongest characteristic, and if any incident or event put us in a bad light, she corrected it. I remember her calmly but firmly telling my brother Cliff, who in his younger days went through a period of over-indulgence and drank to excess, "Don't you act like a drunken Indian in front of us, when it's bad enough the people in town already think we're all drunken Indians." Her words were brought home to me one summer morning. After a night of youthful exuberance, some friends and I hadn't managed to get home and had slept in a car I'd bought with my summer earnings. It was parked in town outside the Manitou Lodge, a well-known watering hole. We awoke to loud banging on the window. It was early, probably 7:30 or 8:00. I don't know why we were parked outside a bar; we were too young to be inside a place that sold liquor, so couldn't have been in there the night before. Anyway, the banging woke me out of my stupor, and the door flew open as soon as I unlocked it.

It was Mom, or I should say her purse, that brought me to full attention as she whaled away at my arms while I tried to protect the rest of my body, including my throbbing head. There were no screams or yelling, merely louder than usual exclamations of disappointment and warnings that someone would probably call the police on us. I'd never seen such disappointment in Mom as on that day.

I don't remember being told about my birth, but it must have been a time of shock and wonder for Mom and Dad as well as my grandparents, when I entered the world eight years after the last of my three older siblings. Cliff, Leon and Marie would most likely have missed my birth, as they'd have just gone back to residential school for the year.

Two girls, Georgina and Marjory, were born within three years of my birth. A third, Shirley (Snooks), was born a year after Marjory entered residential school, mirroring the pattern of Marie and me. I've often wondered if their children's internment created an "empty-nest syndrome" for my parents. Many families on the reserve had similar birth patterns. After the youngest child had gone away to residential school, parents usually had another child within a year, and three or more after that.

The love and affection I received from Kookum (Grandmother) Therese and Mishoom (Grandfather) "Schall" were special. Grandpa's real name was Charles. As I learned English, I came to understand how our forefathers played on words and names. It often arose from the pronunciation of names by the French priests—it was their pronunciation of "Charles" that led to "Schall."

Although Cliff, Leon and Marie, and all the cousins I knew, were in awe and a bit afraid of Mishoom because of his strictness, he was kind and gentle with me. Having already experienced residential school, the others may have mistaken his teasing, sarcasm and gruffness for the heavy-handedness at school that usually resulted in consequences not normally associated with family life. I, on the other hand, welcomed and looked forward to his teasing, make-believe gruffness and invitations to his and Kookum's house for bannock and cake.

Mishoom and I became closely connected just by being together. I recall touching his rough, well-worked and weathered hands as he untangled our catch from his fishnet at the creek. Occasionally he'd fire a ball of snuff from his mouth— "phfft"—turning his head away and directing his tobacco missile away from our morning cache.

I remember his holler clearly. I'd be playing outside near home. Mishoom would be walking on the road toward the bush and the Hudson's Bay store. As he spied me at our house he'd call, "*Umbay, chiboy!* (Come on, big boy!) *Wee chee shin!* (Come with me!)" He'd be on his way to check snares and a couple of traps. Away I'd fly, and Mishoom and I would retrieve rabbits and partridges. I'd watch and listen as he showed me how to skin and stretch a fur in preparation for drying. I looked forward to the end of a week when I'd help him remove the drying furs from their stretchers, pack them in his packsack and head to the store with him.

There he would negotiate and argue with the store manager about price. I somehow lost my capacity to do that in my later years, when I had to discuss wood prices with the paper mill. The residential school experience had destroyed the confidence in negotiating that I'd learned from watching Mishoom. My memories of him go back 60 years or so, but they remain clear in my mind. Many small incidents like these from my pre-residential school years have become clear in my healing journey.

Mom's grandfather Niizhotay spent most of his life in the wilds of the Canadian Shield and had various camping sites on the shore of Lake Winnipeg and along the trails on his trapline between Fort Alexander (Sagkeeng) and Manigotagan.

Uncle Albert, who died in 2008 at age 94, told me it was rumoured that the missionaries asked Niizhotay who had named the small community Manigotagan, and why. Niizhotay initially told them that the Indians and mixed-bloods who'd settled there were a joyous people who enjoyed fiddle music and hooting and hollering after a hard day's work of trapping and fishing. The exuberant people who led the usual celebration could be heard from miles away. A passing trapper heard the commotion and exclaimed to his companion, "*Man i go ta gan!* (That's an awful noise!)" Apparently he didn't think much of the hooting and hollering, particularly that of an off-tune male singer, although the joviality brought joy to the area. I'm not sure the missionaries believed the story, but when baptizing the Indians they subsequently translated the name of the place Manigotagan and anglicized it as Bad Throat.

Another version of the story, told to a different uncle of mine by an old friend and passed on to me, was that Niizhotay named the community. He and a companion had finished their day on the trapline and stopped for the night at a campsite on the shores of Lake Winnipeg. As they drank their tea and smoked their pipes they suddenly heard a broken-down and desperate moose call coming from where some of our people had established a community. They assumed that somehow the moose had gotten a piece of twig or remnants of his evening meal stuck in his throat—that or he had eaten too many chokecherries and was having difficulty getting rid of them. Even though Niizhotay and his companion weren't known for any musical tendencies, they recognized the sound as unnatural and decided *man i go ta gan*—"this sound is bad."

Although in their baptismal reports the missionaries began referring to the community as Bad Throat, Indian and Métis people continued to call it Manigotagan. My uncle was very pleased that the attempt by the missionaries to anglicize the name had failed.

OLDER SIBLINGS

Clifford, my oldest sibling, was born in 1927. I only saw him during summer holidays. As a young boy, Cliff was a free spirit and had the most difficulty of all of us living at residential school and being away from home. His fiery anger at being locked up led the priests to suggest to Mom and Dad that Cliff could better help the family at home. Happily for him, he was thus allowed to leave school in Grade 3.

As he got older, Cliff travelled the area doing various jobs and fell into a life of mischief and self-indulgence. At 20, still not of legal age and with the Indian Act still not recognizing him as a person, he joined the Royal Winnipeg Rifles of the Canadian Forces. We don't know much about his stint in the army, but we do know he was discharged for saluting incorrectly—with his left hand—and getting into too many scraps.

His love of fun and drinking was initially admired. As time went on, though, stories and rumours surfaced about his exploits and his reputation began to sour. I recall stories of people at dances, movies and other public places yelling or exclaiming, "Cliff is coming!" anticipating him instigating a commotion. He quit drinking at 27 and went on to enjoy 35 years of sober and productive living.

He was a bachelor, a favourite among his many nieces and nephews and a fixture at community events. He was proud of his sobriety and long affiliation with Alcoholics Anonymous. I still have his small, well-used copy of *One Day at a Time*. In 1991 Cliff was admitted to hospital. He'd been diagnosed years earlier with Lou Gehrig's disease but had withheld that information to spare his family heartache. Suffering the gradual disabling effects of the disease over many years, Cliff endured it alone, living with courage and independence to the end. He died on December 10, 1991.

Leon, my parents' second-oldest child, attended residential school for eight years and thrived in cadet activities in the three or four years that the school had this program. He enlisted in Princess Patricia's Canadian Light Infantry at age 18. Like Cliff, he wasn't yet recognized as a person under the Indian Act although he served his country in Korea. It wasn't until 1960 that Indians in Canada were recognized as human beings under the Indian Act and given the right to vote.

Leon was wounded in Korea and spent time in seven hospitals before arriving at Deer Lodge Hospital in Winnipeg in June 1951. A report of his being missing in action had been clipped out and posted on a bulletin board in my playroom at residential school. I remember being proud that my brother was recognized but shocked to see the notice. His recovery from war injuries was long and difficult, but he managed to get his journeyman plumbing and pipe-fitting papers during this time and devoted himself to his family.

Leon too succumbed to the ravages of the bottle in his early adulthood, as he battled the effects and memories of both trench warfare and eight years at residential school. As he climbed the healing ladder, he was honoured as a First Nations veteran and flag-bearer at many conferences and events. I used to watch him with pride, and I can still enjoy seeing his proud march on a video of Remembrance Day in Ottawa.

Marie, the youngest of my parents' initial trio of children, attended residential school for about eight years. Of all the children, she was the rock and steady influence in our family life on the reserve. When Mom and Dad both worked, Marie took over parenting duties and even gave up her career as a lab technician to be closer to Mom and Dad and to help at home.

Marie is the strongest individual I know in dealing with residential school experiences. The school's effects on her were less visible, and because she worked with quiet strength after leaving there, I assumed she was invincible in handling life's shortcomings and that nothing significant had happened to her at school. But then she precipitated an abuse claim against the federal government and the Roman Catholic Church and hired a lawyer. Not knowing the nature of her claim, I went to the legal hearing to join her for lunch afterwards. As she emerged from the hearing with her lawyer, I was stunned to see her visibly in shock, angry and tear-stained, and hear her exclaim that she was going home. I sank onto the waiting-room couch and asked her to sit with me. She eventually determined to finish the hearing process. I spent the rest of the afternoon in the waiting room. Her healing process had begun.

During her subsequent turmoil and the breakup of her marriage, Marie lived in a little trailer away from the reserve. She attended some healing sessions during this time to deal with her marriage breakup. These sessions helped her understand that her residential school experiences were the cause of most of the problems within her marriage. She now enjoys her own home back on the reserve at the same point of land where we grew up. Five of her six children live within walking distance and see her almost daily. She is in contact with all her children and half a dozen grandchildren, and she is contented.

EARLY MORNINGS
WITH ALFRED MANN

The comfort of waking in my own bed to the sounds of birds, frogs, crickets and other wildlife is all I'd ever known until I went to Fort Alexander Indian Residential School. Sometimes, after waking up before dawn and sitting and chatting with Mom in the kitchen, and as other family members awakened, I'd slip out into the early morning with my trusty old slingshot and wander toward the river and along its forested banks.

Of the three or four houses between our house and the school was one where my Uncle Charlie lived, built with the help of Grandpa, Dad and other uncles. It was near the creek leading to Adams Store, which used to be the Hudson's Bay store. To the east of our house, going toward town, my grandparents lived for years in the home Grandpa built, near the forest and away from the river. Uncle Albert and his family lived with them there. Just beyond my grandparents' house and nearer the river, across from Treaty Point, lived a dear friend and elder, Alfred Mann. As he lived next to Grandpa and Grandma's, I visited him and Harriet, his wife, often.

Alfred's nearest neighbour in the direction of Pine Falls was Aunt Irene, her husband, Old Joe Gus, and their family, including my cousin Dee, or Dee-ainse ("small Dee"). Next to their house by the river lived Ralph Alexander and his family. Ralph's parents lived 500 feet farther on. I also occasionally spent time with Ralph's boys Percy, John and Harvey, swimming and playing by Treaty Point.

A mile nearer town lived my other close cousins, nine boys and two girls, and their parents, Dad's brother J.B. and his wife, Agnes. I rarely saw the other relatives who lived in between, John Fontaine and John Thompson, until I was older. John was one of our earliest chiefs and often visited Alfred and my grandparents, sometimes when I was there. I enjoyed the contact with all these neighbours.

In my small world I knew and was close to almost all of my uncles, aunts, cousins and my parents' cousins, and I spent a huge amount of time with my grandparents, particularly Schall and Therese. Although Mom and Dad visited other people related to us, I didn't have close contact with or remember them because we only saw them at church on Sundays.

Alfred was neither an uncle nor a cousin and also not Roman Catholic, so he had little contact with the church on the reserve. I was fortunate to know him because he was a close neighbour. Much later I learned that he and others from the Anglican side of the reserve in fact were cousins of my mom, as my great-grandfather Niizhotay was related to some Anglican members on the reserve.

Mom had lost her closeness with her father's side of the family; going to school when she was only four or five had completely alienated her from knowledge of them. I think the church and school destroyed almost completely her memory of her Indian heritage and family. In any case, I didn't know for a long time that Alfred was kin and that our closeness wasn't just that of an old man and a young boy but a blood relationship.

In the bush and along the shore, traversing the rocky outcrops and forests of my world, I'd make my rounds, checking snares and traps and tirelessly exploring Treaty Point. Then I'd emerge in view of Alfred's house. As I came up the hill and headed home, he often called me over to his place. He'd be sitting in his rocking chair on his front veranda and enjoying an early-morning pipe. Sometimes the tobacco's aroma would drift down to the point.

"*Ahneen, chiboy* (Hello, big boy)," he'd holler. "*Umbay pi mooch cheyan* (Come and visit)." My young legs would quickly carry me to his side. I'll always remember the sweet, strong smell of his pipe tobacco and the smouldering smudge, which sat on an uncovered iron pot. Without fail he'd enthusiastically ask me about my snares, if I'd met wild chicken or partridges, and *"Anday sheesheebuck nipeeng?* (Where are the ducks on the water?)"

The cleansing smudge would slowly rise and mingle with the smoke from his tobacco and then flutter out into the clear morning air. If I were lucky enough to have had the Creator guide a *wapoose* or *pinnay* (rabbit or partridge) into one of my snares, Alfred would take that treasure and put it into his wooden storage box until it was time for me to head home.

On these mornings I enjoyed two breakfasts. "Harriet!" he'd holler toward the open screened door. *"Ashum a kee sayns* (Feed the little boy)." She'd emerge shortly with a fresh cookie or two and hot bannock wrapped in a square blue-and-red-checkered towel. She'd put these delicacies on a wooden stool beside Alfred, asking me how Mom and Dad were. She'd refill Alfred's teacup and bring me a cool beverage, probably Kool-Aid. I'd dig in even though I'd just had some of Mom's fresh bannock and would do so again when I got home. I never refused Harriet's baking or steaming hot porridge.

Mom and Dad were delighted when I described such visits, particularly how Alfred would graciously share and savour his bannock, jam and porridge. They'd laugh when I described splashes of porridge and bannock crumbs clinging to his beard. They laughed, I realized, because I too would have bits of porridge and bannock on parts of my face and the front of my T-shirt. I never told Alfred that his nice bushy beard and moustache had crumbs and splashes of porridge on them. I smile to myself and feel deep love for him and Harriet as I recall her tossing him a faded old towel so he could clean off his breakfast. That beard remains prominent in my memory and I can still feel its bushy massage against my cheek.

As I got older, and misguided from being at residential school for some time, my visits with them during summer holidays became less frequent. When I went there one summer years later, Alfred and Harriet's house was abandoned and boarded up. I never saw them again and don't remember where they went or what happened to them, but I think of them often with both pleasure and sadness, remembering how lucky I was to have had such a loving and carefree relationship with them.

They come to mind now on my trips to Fort Alexander, which has been renamed informally, using its original Ojibway name, as Sagkeeng First Nation. I reminisce with Percy Alexander and we chuckle at our memories, especially of Alfred and his beard and of Percy's family's nearest neighbour, Old Joe Gus.

Old Joe, Dee's father, was often described as having an unmatched work ethic. Our parents and others of their generation often said that he would be found dead one day, still standing upright with 25-foot lengths of wood on his shoulder and in mid-stride on the road to home, but having departed into the spirit world.

M Y   D A D ,   M Y   H E R O

One special clear memory of my early years is of a Sunday morning when everyone was getting ready to go to church and I was running around being a nuisance. The sky was clear except for a few fluffy white clouds outlined against the deep blue sea of the sky and moving along briskly in a nice, warm breeze. Mom was in the kitchen doing something last-minute. She was obviously ready to go and already wearing her "white ladies hat," as my brothers and sister called it. They (and I later) called her Lady Jane when she wore it. The description came from a magazine Marie kept under her mattress.

Mom had got the kitchen ready for visitors who'd stop in for a meal or a snack after Mass. Marie was somewhere getting ready, and I don't know where my brothers were. They'd have been in their teens then, so perhaps they were out working somewhere for the summer. This must have been during summer holidays for residential school kids, as it was early or mid-summer and it was rare that we were all home.

Dad was standing in front of the wash basin in the main living area of the house. Having had a wash, he was shaving in his white sleeveless undershirt. I remember looking in awe at his muscular, smooth physique, honed from years of hard physical labour as head sawyer at the mill. He was splashing and lathering his face using a little brush, which he periodically swished around in a bowl to make more lather for his chin, neck and cheeks.

Suddenly he whirled around and peered intently outside to the meadow bordering the forest beyond the road. He'd spotted something in the mirror and his instincts were on high alert. He suddenly dropped everything into the basin, grabbed a towel and, as he rushed into his and Mom's bedroom, brushed the foam and water from his face. He emerged, still in what might now be called a muscle shirt, gripping his shotgun and yelling to Mom that he'd catch up with us.

He'd seen a deer meandering across the field, grazing just beyond the road. I remember that her coat wasn't yet crimson, which it would have been in late summer or early fall, and she was fat enough that it was surely beyond late spring, when deer are still shaggy, spotty grey and skinny. Dad scrambled and crouched in the slight incline of the ditch behind the doe. The wind was almost directly in front of him, so he had to approach the doe so that she didn't smell or hear him.

Mom hurried us kids along and off we went. I know she enjoyed having extra time at church before Mass to visit and pray and meditate. We seemed to be moving at an unusually fast pace, though, and I kept turning back to try and see Dad. I wished he'd just shoot the deer and then catch up with us.

Suddenly there was a loud, faraway bang. Even though we were already some distance away, I knew exactly what he'd done and that he planned to haul the animal home with the help of relatives after church. Having learned from him, I knew that he'd slit the animal's throat, removed the sweat glands and placed the carcass on a slight incline to drain the blood. He'd have opened up the carcass and covered it with grass, small trees and branches.

There were always other people on the road as we went to church; some we'd pass, and some we would see in the distance, walking ahead of us. Some Sundays, a family might pass us in a horse-drawn buggy. But not this day. Mom was moving us along smartly, and my skipping had become more of a jog. It wasn't far to the church, and we always got there fairly quickly. Today, with Mom in control, we probably cut the time by 10 percent, as we didn't stop to visit with people along the way as Dad did. As we passed the store, I tried to delay our march by walking backward and looking for Dad.

It was well into Mass when Dad walked in and joined us. He had on his black suit and open-necked white shirt and carried his usual black hat with the small red feather in the hatband. He was slightly flushed and smiled at friends and relatives to right and left. He knelt at his usual place at the end of our pew. My chest was pounding and I was anxious and excited to tell everyone what Dad had done.

I didn't even consider that the deer might have escaped. I felt the little drum inside my chest pushing forward, as I knew we were in for a treat in the next few days. My dad was the best and truly a great man, one who took care of his family and relatives. I knew the deer would fill many bellies and that Dad would be inundated with questions about the exact details of his kill. Some would wonder about the size of the slug he'd designed himself for his shotgun.

The walk home, I remember, was very casual for all the churchgoers. Friends and relatives were busy chatting about the past week's activities and their plans for the coming week. Dad and Uncle Albert picked up the pace and left the group behind. Mom walked with Granny and a couple of sisters-in-law and their children, the young ones skipping and playing tag. Older cousins walked more deliberately and talked in a subdued tone about things I didn't understand. I thought they were boring.

My short legs worked hard, trying to keep up to Dad. I wanted to help with butchering and was already feeling the warmth of the deer as the organs—liver, heart and other delicacies—came out of the chest cavity. Dad often let me probe inside an animal's cavity and remove organs. Alas, I don't remember this episode beyond that point; I just remember the joy and completeness of that day.

BLUEBERRY DAYS

Each summer, before any of them owned cars or trucks, Dad and some of his brothers packed up their families and hired vehicles, used their boats or loaded us all on the old Canadian National Railway to take us blueberry picking. These ventures took us to various parts of Manitoba and also into Ontario, where we'd live in the woods for weeks at a time. Although Dad worked full-time, every year he'd leave his job to ensure that the family could pick blueberries. There weren't many head sawyers at the mill; I used to think it was closed when Dad was gone.

Families set up campsites like little villages in the blueberry area. Most years they were at a place called Belair. A Mr. and Mrs. Green owned and operated the community store there; it was only accessible by forest roads through the area's sandhills. Our tent villages existed for weeks every year. Mr. Green and his family encouraged them, providing water and toilet facilities, and became lifelong friends of people who returned year after year to earn money picking and selling blueberries. Whole families participated. Dad managed all of our family's activities, coordinating site selection and setting it up so we could live comfortably.

He and a couple of his brothers always travelled together with their families on these money-making ventures, which included rice gathering in the fall and pulp cutting in the winter and spring. Uncle J.B. had a pulp-cutting camp on the eastern shore of Lake Winnipeg that provided jobs for many families. We preschoolchildren thrived in the freedom and camaraderie of these camps.

The mess halls were run mostly by Mom and my aunts. They had a wide array of fine food to feed the hard workers and their children, who needed energy to play and to help with chores like setting and checking rabbit traps and snares and hunting ptarmigan. Rabbit stew, soup and bannock were staples, and little guys like me learned to help provide nourishment to the whole camp.

Almost every night at the camp you could hear the whining of the fiddle, the twang of the guitar and the rhythmic stomping of jigging feet. This, of course, was all the more exciting and enticing because of the hooting, hollering, yelling and laughing that came with square dances. Certain voices became easily identified, and local reputations were made in the camps. The square-dance caller was like an auctioneer with his rapid-fire directions to dancers.

The security and safety of being tucked in feather robes inside our tents was sometimes too much for us to bear, and we'd succumb to the merriment and sneak out to watch. Looking back, I suspect we were given chances to watch, our parents knowing we'd enjoy the festivities and not get underfoot. They knew we wouldn't stray because we didn't want to get lost. They also knew we thought we were getting away with something.

Usually the older folks—grandparents, mothers, fathers, friends and other relatives—sat outside the tents, smoking, drinking tea and visiting. Many times they'd call for us young ones to come and sit with them beside the fire, and they'd tell us family stories about ghosts, devils and such mischief-makers in the Ojibway culture as Weendigo and Weeskayjak. The crackling of sparks and the soft hissing of flames from the fires are etched in my mind.

We'd listen enraptured and awestruck as the elders imparted their wisdom. We learned why ducks waddle, why muskrats and beavers build dams, why the willow is red. I often wondered why we never got to see Weeskayjak. Every aspect and explanation of nature, of why things were, were attributed to him. Our imaginations were as free and wild as those animals of the forest that we imagined were hunched just behind the edge of the dancing firelight.

Evenings would become quiet as midnight approached. Eventually there'd be complete quiet except for the occasional snap and crackle of dying fires being put out, usually by the heads of families. Young adults, dancing and celebrating their freedom, knew that as daybreak approached the eastern sky would announce another blueberry-picking day. Sleep would be gone as elders and family heads awakened the whole camp.

Days began early. The blueberry buyers' trucks took us to the berry patches. They left early, so if you were late you had to pick berries close to the tent village, along with the elders. A site probably had 20 or 25 tents, and the first areas to be picked out were the ones nearby. If you wanted to make money, you had to pick three or four baskets a day, and you couldn't do that if you slept in. If you missed the truck ride, time would be wasted walking to the prime picking areas with baskets, water, food and whatever else you needed.

We spent whole days out in the pines, sometimes miles from camp. Mom always packed food, blankets, Kool-Aid and other necessities. Dad made sure that canvas, rope and other paraphernalia were included. Mom packed enough food for a mid-morning snack, noon lunch and afternoon snack. The meals were unforgettable, especially the desserts that Dad insisted be included in every lunch sack.

My brothers needed huge amounts of food, particularly Leon. At home and at other gathering places, Leon had an unequalled reputation as an eater and lover of food, especially pies. Dad always said with a proud grin that "his boy had a straight pipe," which caused him to have such a huge appetite. Leon also became a legend in the family and community because of how many meals he could eat on New Year's Day—a day of visiting and being offered a meal at every house. I think he holds the record on our reserve for the number of meals and raisin pies eaten on New Year's Day. When he was serving in Korea he marvelled at how people there survived almost exclusively on rice. His thoughts over there were as much about Mom's cooking as about staying alive.

Dad would pick a shady, breezy spot among short and medium-sized pines and cover the meal pack with boughs, branches and blankets. Mom used blankets as tablecloths and also to make a rest area. Dad would find a piece of long, dry tamarack, tie a pillowcase to one end and secure it to a tall pine. This served as a marker for our spot.

Often Dad and other family members succumbed at noon to the chattering of chipmunks, the chirping of chickadees and the soft swishing of poplar trees as the breeze tirelessly blew its soothing, refreshing breath into all of nature. These naps were short but relaxing. Sometimes I dozed in Mom's lap or watched the soft up-and-down movement of Dad's barrel chest. Mom always said he could sleep anywhere, any time. He was a contented man.

The day ended with a truck arriving at a specified meeting place and families loading up their belongings and boxes packed with blueberries, secured in canvas packsacks, for the trip home to the campsite. Kids with blue lips and mouths, stings, bites and rashes would be clamouring and scrambling about. We all enjoyed unloading the day's haul. Usually my contribution was rewarded with a couple of treats from the camp store. The most memorable was a toffee bar and an Orange Crush, which came in a bottle with grooves on its side. My consumption of many toffee bars and my seeming always to have one on hand earned me the nickname "Taffy," which some people still use.

Blueberry picking was done mostly in what is now a forest reserve nestled between sandhills and little valleys, with pockets of small marshes. Muskeg tea from this area was a treat. The aroma of it would filter through the forest soon after the pickers set up camp. The hot, fine sand toughened our feet if we stayed out without shoes or runners, and we'd go home with a good tan as well.

I still visit the forest reserve often and marvel at its beauty, which is enhanced by the glittering, dancing leaves of the tall poplars, the lively birch, the chokecherry and saskatoon berry bushes, the bright-red pin cherry trees and the cranberry bushes with their brilliant orange berries.

WILD RICE / LIFE LESSONS

Mom and Dad picked rice every year at Rice Lake or Lone Island Lake and took me with them. Like blueberry picking, this was an annual tradition for our family and others. The parents had equal roles in this venture. One would push-pole or paddle the canoe in and out of thick patches of wild rice while the other, usually the woman, knocked the rice into the canoe, aiming to get maximum results and not knock rice into the river. Dad used to brag that Mom was unmatched in the art of rice threshing and rice picking.

The weeks spent picking rice conjure good memories of adventure and exploration. I vaguely remember as a little guy being with Mom and Dad in a canoe in the rice field. Sitting near the front of the canoe, I had to wear a peaked cap with a red plaid handkerchief attached to its back to protect me from the rice coming off the sticks that Mom expertly manoeuvred. My turning to watch her threshing slowed her down considerably, as she had to be extra careful not to hit me or have me stung by flying rice. I admired how she swung her tools as the rice swished into the canoe.

I have no idea where I might have seen a drummer, but Mom reminded me of one as she worked, expertly bending the stalks of the wild rice over the side of the canoe with one stick and threshing them with another. The threshers she used were each about three feet long and an inch in diameter at the top, narrowing down to about half an inch at the tip. They were made from either dried tamarack or pine. Dad, being a perfectionist, made the finest threshers and spent a lot of time scraping and filing his. They had to be inspected and approved by Mom to be sure they had just the right balance.

Some jaunts were intended as quick training sessions for me and others. On these occasions, I usually sat in the bottom of the middle of the canoe. Sometimes Mom gave me the paddle beside her so that I could paddle with Dad, or she'd show me how to whack the rice. Sometimes I just watched them picking and we'd stop at a landing on the river to enjoy a refreshing drink and perhaps some sweets. Near mid-afternoon, pickers docked at the landing with their caches of rice, and as incoming canoes were spotted, non-pickers—mostly little kids and their babysitters—congregated to greet families and friends. If a canoe was sitting low in the water, it meant a lot of rice had been picked. Pickers had to manoeuvre carefully not to spill any.

I would watch with pride as Mom and Dad pulled in with only an inch or two between the top of their canoe and the water. Often they returned early to stow the rice in specially constructed bags; if they were early enough, they sometimes returned to the river or lake to get more rice or took me along to explore the area in preparation for the next day's activities.

Non-pickers spent the days with cousins and canine friends, exploring waterways and rocks and cliffs, hunting partridge, rabbit and other small animals, and chasing squirrels. We'd also climb rocks and hills, go swimming, pick berries and nuts, run from imaginary bears and chase porcupines and skunks. Often we ventured out in a canoe to explore the river, away from the pickers. We'd spend an hour or two doing that, picking our own wild rice by hand, not yet confident or strong enough to venture into the thick growth. This contribution, of course, didn't go unrewarded, as we'd usually pick enough to warrant treats.

Sometimes we'd find a swimming hole and all of us boys and the dogs would swim, then spend part of the day removing bloodsuckers from various parts of our bodies. Sometimes Copenhagen snuff, a tobacco used instead of cigarettes and deposited under the tongue, found its way into someone's possession; it was an excellent sucker remover.

This was a trick I'd learned from Uncle J.B. in an encounter with bloodsuckers during a blueberry-picking trip at Redditt Lake, a shallow lake in northwestern Ontario and home to many bloodsuckers. I'd wandered away from other family members into an area of these little critters one hot, humid day. Uncle J.B. found me atop a rock by the lake trying to remove the little devils from my leg. He dug under his tongue and rubbed snuff directly onto a sucker. It immediately started to wriggle, released its grip and fell off. I think he was joking when he suggested I carry a can of snuff with me all the time. I found the procedure effective on wood ticks as well. I never did acquire a taste for snuff, though— I remember feeling faint and regurgitating a small wad after accidentally swallowing it.

In 1948, the year I was to go to school, Dad decided to have me stay with the family past the start of the school year. I imagine there'd been no question for him about my going rice picking as in previous years. I don't know whether he was making a statement by keeping me away until past the start. I expect he rationalized his decision by telling himself and Mom that he wanted me to learn how to survive in the bush and how to make a living as a picker. He was quite silent in matters involving his children except when he could provide mentorship and leadership. He'd bring me to school when he was good and ready.

The extra time I spent that year rice picking—living in the outdoors, eating meals cooked on an open fire, sitting perched on a tree stump or crossed-legged by the fire—is one of the outstanding memories I have carried with me.

BUSH-CAMP ADVENTURES

Uncle J.B. and Dad were two of nine brothers. According to Granny, Dad took J.B. under his wing almost immediately after he was born. Being similar in personality and work ethic, they enjoyed partnering in various ventures. Mom told me that Dad sometimes adjusted his activities in order to be with and work with J.B. In the 1940s, when J.B. established a pulp-cutting operation to employ our own people and to sell pulpwood to the mill, Dad temporarily left his employment to work at the bush camp and help J.B. make the operation successful.

I don't remember much about the pulp-cutting camps, maybe because as young children we didn't engage in the actual work as we did with the blueberry-picking and rice-gathering ventures. I *do* remember sitting around the mess kitchen as we watched our mothers prepare meals, "cleaning" pots and pans with our fingers as we devoured leftover chocolate or baking.

I also remember cousins Dennis and Purvis and me riding on sleighs stacked 8 to 10 feet high with pulpwood. We'd jump off into piles of snow along the road. These jumps turned into competitions to see who could leap the farthest. We learned to jump off close to a bend in the road so as to catch up with the sleigh without becoming exhausted. The driver had to slow down at the bends to avoid a catastrophe such as dumping a load of pulp. I wonder now how it was that one of us wasn't impaled on a stump, tree or branch hidden in the snow. If our parents had known about our fun, the sleigh drivers would have been in deep horse poop.

I remember the steaming horses and their smell as they worked their way along the snow-packed trails toward a pick-up point for the wood, which was destined for the paper mill in Pine Falls, about 10 miles from camp. This is where Dad and some of his brothers worked at various times, but when I was a young boy listening to Dad and his brothers and friends, it seemed that people from the reserve were purposely not being hired to work there. Managers at the Pine Falls mill hired everyone but Indian boys, and they also sought out young men from other towns and the rural area to play for their all-white baseball and hockey teams. Only a handful of our people were eventually given chances to earn a living in the mill. Then supervisors bragged about who had the "best Indian worker."

Over time, attitudes at the mill changed toward acceptance of reserve workers, as Dad and others proved their worth. Mill managers and supervisors acknowledged years later that there were clearly managerial and leadership candidates among Indian employees, but they never held positions other than as labourers. Dad worked for almost 30 years as head sawyer but never as foreman of the sawyers.

The bush camp was basically run by the women partners of the cutters. They did the hiring and firing and ensured that the wonderful mess hall where you could have a snack or meal any time, the family quarters and the singles bunkhouses all ran smoothly. I often wondered why the bunkhouses were watched so closely by mothers and other women; I realized years later that not all the women were attached to men at the camp. I don't remember any great catastrophes or scandals because of that, though, and I imagine some lifelong partnerships were established in spite of Mom's and others' vigilance.

One memory surfaces and lingers of a camp worker who used to tease us and enjoy our youthful exuberance at the cutting site and, especially, when he was driving a team of horses. Although other drivers enjoyed our play and company, Alfredense ("young, or small, Alfred") enjoyed our company most. He'd yell, laugh and almost yodel with joy. If he hadn't been the responsible guy he was, he'd have let us drive the horses while he competed in seeing who could jump the farthest. His trick of slapping the behinds of the horses on straight stretches to make us work for our fun got to be a game in itself. Although we'd have loved to drive the team, he never succumbed to the temptation. I don't think he wanted to answer to our parents.

We enjoyed Alfred-ense, and the kibitzing and teasing was reciprocal. Sometimes, perhaps because he'd had evening chores or had had a nip with other workers, he stayed in the bunkhouse a while after breakfast and we assumed that he was resting. We'd throw snowballs at his window or scratch on it and then run away. We'd push our toques as far down as possible and bring our scarves up over the bridge of our noses so that only our eyes were visible, and then build a step from mounds of snow and peek into his bunk area. I don't know if we ever startled him; mostly he reacted vigorously and scared us instead. I'm sure sometimes he almost broke the glass of the window. I'm sure also that he was a pretty good actor.

One morning he was particularly fast visiting the mess area, but slow coming out of the bunkhouse after breakfast. Dennis and I decided to start his day with a scare and snuck a view through the window. What we saw was the most confusing sight I'd come upon to that point. We were both speechless and I'm sure our lower jaws rested on our little chests. There was Alfred with his arms around one of the cleaning ladies, and his mouth was on her mouth as they embraced. His nose was pressed to her cheek and her eyes were closed. We almost fell flat on our faces as we got out of there as fast as we could. We weren't sure whether he'd seen us or not, and the twinkle in his eye and sly smile later also bewildered us.

We didn't lose any kinship with Alfred-ense after that, and in fact I think he delighted in our attempts to tease him about it. Years later, when we were in residential school, we learned that he and Joanne had actually been courting then and did eventually marry. I rarely saw him after I went to school, only once or twice at church; he was probably busy raising a family.

I saw Alfred nearly 45 years later at a retirement home in Selkirk, a town on the Winnipeg River north of Winnipeg. I didn't have a chance to spend time with him then, but 10 years later I did. He recalled driving the teams of horses at the camp, and his eyes and expression changed as he, too, remembered what a happy time it was. I was sad to learn that he and Joanne had parted company a few years after the winter I'd seen them together at the bush camp. He talked about his neighbours and the upcoming visit of a nurse to the retirement home. He told me with pride about his daughter's visits and how she cleaned and washed his suite. He was proud of her and her husband. "She's married to Happy Smith's son," he boasted. Alfred-ense was now one of our elders, and I was sad that the happy time we both recalled was so far in the past. I left his bachelor condo with a heavy heart.

Memories of happy times surfaced a lot in my first year at school, particularly at night and in the dark. Eventually they came less and less often—perhaps mercifully, for whimpering and crying were reason for the older boys to belittle and abuse the younger ones—and later I thought perhaps they were only a dream.

Fortunately, my healing journey has enabled me to treasure these remembered moments, and I have smiled, laughed and, yes, cried about them. I think Mom and Dad, and my departed siblings, smile down at me as I become more and more the spirited, carefree boy I was.

ON WHOSE AUTHORITY?

The residential school system was established in Fort Alexander in 1905. Dad, born in 1900, was among its first students. Although he learned to read and write, he wasn't there long. Parents then had more control and say over the fate of their children and saw the need for only basic skills like reading, writing and arithmetic.

The Church hadn't yet established control over the community, and families provided for and brought up their children. Paid work in the Fort Alexander area was minimal, so our people were busy for months working at various locations away from the reserve. I've heard numerous stories of individuals from other reserves being required to get permission from Indian agents to leave their reserves, but Fort Alexander Indians never encountered an agent with the audacity to curtail their movements.

There are many stories of our grandparents, uncles and cousins travelling to other parts of the province in search of work or to pursue traditional activities on traditional territorial lands.

Moise, my great-grandfather, had established his independence prior to the 1871 signing of Treaty 1. He and his family, and those who followed, kept this independence even after reserve boundaries were established when the 1876 survey was completed. His nine children, including my grandfather Schall, continued to enjoy their freedom even after the arrival of the Roman Catholic Church.

I recall a story told at a family gathering that demonstrates the independence and straightforwardness of Grandpa Schall. When residential schools were first incorporated into First Nations communities, Schall and Therese wanted their children educated. The eighth child, Tony, better known as Ah twain (perhaps a derivative of his full name, Antoine), being young, somehow got a reprimand from the priest one day. When Schall learned that Tony had been assaulted by the priest, he marched over to the school from his home about two miles away. Father G. greeted him with "Bonjour, Schall," thinking this was a friendly visit. Schall retorted, "Fuck you, bonjour, you hit my boy!" I don't know the outcome. Schall was a good, kind and religious man and was never in the habit of using such words, but after this experience his family had no need of further confrontations.

Schall tried to instill his independence and freethinking in his 13 children, including Dad. Thus they were very independent and had gone against almost every policy and law forced on Indian people by government officials and the Church. In those early years, Dad and his brothers seldom attended community or band meetings, as they felt they were controlled and conducted for the benefit of the government and the Church, not the community.

I'm sad now to think that Dad eventually succumbed to the system and quietly surrendered to the notion that the government controlled Indian people and that the Department of Indian Affairs was the "boss." Steady work at the mill meant he no longer had to be away from the family for long, but it also meant he was more accessible, and he was slowly drawn into Church activities. With increased involvement, he was subjected to Church teachings.

It's unfortunate that Mom and Dad, because of their residential school experiences and the Church's presence in the community, became not only God-fearing but also *Church*-fearing. The respect and awe in which our people held the clergy was mostly based on fear of damnation and the devil. Clergy took advantage of it. The Church's word became God's word, no matter how wrong or misdirected the word was that came from the priests and nuns. Their agenda was to satisfy their contract with the government to establish power and control over our people. These preachers and soul-gatherers, after all, knew nothing about who we were, and were ignorant of our culture and deep spiritual beliefs. Our spirituality became less of an influence on our people as our Creator was replaced by a punishing God.

LESSONS IN FEAR

Mom and Dad's wishes and justification for my attending residential school were confusing for Mom. Knowing me, and having seen me grow and be a part of her, was a natural and joyful experience for her. She'd had no experience of growing up with her own mother and knew only residential school life until her marriage to Dad. She'd lost three children to residential school before me and didn't want to lose more. Still, she strongly believed that attending residential school would allow me to succeed in a white person's world.

She also feared the Church and its teachings. She didn't want to offend the priests and nuns and feared excommunication, and so was persuaded to believe that having her children under the Church's exclusive authority was what the Creator wanted. She thought that Church officials and their helpers were infallible.

Unwavering conviction like hers made it easier for the federal government and the Church to control and weaken our people.

Mom and Dad had never been subjected to Roman Catholic Church teachings before they went to residential school, so everything they heard was new and had to be true, in their eyes, because priests said they represented Jesus Christ and God, who to us was the same as the Creator. Mom and my aunts told stories of sermons that illustrated the dire consequences that could follow if they opposed the Church and its representatives. Two sermons in particular come to mind.

One described a parish member who faithfully attended Mass and received the host through Communion, but never went to confession. You were supposed to go to confession before having Communion. The priests tried to help this man understand the requirement of confession, but to no avail. One Sunday while he walked back to his pew after receiving Communion, as he was looking around and acknowledging friends and neighbours and still eating the host, droplets of bright red blood began to stain his mouth. Then they started to splatter onto his chest. The blood wouldn't stop, and he panicked and made a mad rush to the river to try to wash it away.

Churchgoers found him a few feet from the water. He'd drowned, even though he hadn't reached the water and even though his mouth and clothes were dry and free of bloodstains. The message Mom and others took from this sermon stayed with them: punishment would be quick and harsh if you didn't heed the priests' words. There'd be no forgiveness and no mercy.

A second sermon Mom described concerned the funeral of a good, kind man who'd been much respected. He'd led what appeared to be a good, loving life and had helped his people with kindness. At the funeral, after the priest had blessed the casket with incense and holy water, something strange happened when he turned away to return to the altar. The droplets of holy water he'd sprinkled on the casket began to steam and hiss. As the priest turned around to see what was happening, churchgoers watched in horror as smoke began to seep out of the casket. The priest called for two parishioners to help him open the casket. When they did, the inside burst into flames. The heat was unbearable and affected the whole church almost immediately. People rushed for the door, and in just a few minutes the church was empty.

After a few minutes outside, and seeing no obvious danger coming from within the church, the priest and two parishioners re-entered, only to find the interior calm and clear of smoke and flames. The casket was intact, its lid closed. They approached cautiously and lifted the lid. The casket was empty except for some ashes heaped in the middle of it. Little flashes of hot embers sparked up, but there was no obvious damage. The good man inside had been replaced by the pile of ashes.

It turned out that this man had disagreed with the priest about his children's baptism. He'd insisted that they be baptized later, when it was convenient for him and his family. He'd also argued that the children weren't ready for residential school. There'd been other disagreements about Church matters as well. In his sermon, the priest said the man had been taken by the devil and purposely burned inside the church because of his disobedience and lack of faith.

But beyond the fear the weekly sermons had instilled, Mom believed that our being taken away and kept at school was the only way for us to learn and to compete and succeed in the white world. She would talk to me about books and writing, and in my early years at school I especially enjoyed English and spelling.

However, in my second to last year at the Fort Alexander School, when I was not yet 15, I had an encounter with the boys' supervisor, Brother B., that changed my destiny. I had done something to incur his wrath. In our playroom, there were two flights of stairs leading up to our dormitory. On this night, he stood on the landing at the top of the first flight of stairs as we lined up at the bottom. He slowly and deliberately began his descent, stopping on the first step in front of us. As we stood in line, ready to march up to our dormitory, he barked out his order: "Theodore, come over here!" As he called me to the front of the line, just in front of the smallest boys, he looked like he was 10 feet tall. The fact that he stood on the first step of the staircase made him bigger and scarier.

He stepped down and began sniffing me, first on my shoulders, then on each side of my face. Some of the older boys had introduced us to smoking and we sometimes indulged in a cigarette, or a part of one, even if we didn't enjoy it. The excitement of being able to get away with something that was banned was always too much for us! On this evening, Brother B.'s acute sense of smell found me out.

Suddenly, he swung his right arm back, and with a quick, deliberate whirlwind motion, his clenched fist cracked me across my face, clipping my nose. I tried to swing my face to the left to avoid full contact and protect my nose and eyes. I tumbled backward and down into a heap on the concrete floor, blood gushing down my nose. My right ear and side of my face had taken the brunt of the blow and the pain felt like I had run into an oak baseball bat.

Brother B. left me almost knocked right out on the concrete floor and moved up to the first landing of the stairs. I could see the fear in the eyes of the little boys at the front of the line. Dazed and bewildered, I struggled to my feet, blinking, with my hand on my ear, trying to steady myself and stop the blood. From what seemed far away, a distant voice or whisper came from behind me: "*Ka ka wee cheego* (We'll help you)." Wavering on unsteady feet, I stood up and staggered into the line beside the bigger boys. I stepped onto the first stair, staring up to where Brother B. stood as he watched the boys marching to their dormitories. Through my teary eyes, my bloody nose, the throbbing and ringing in my ear, I saw him catch my murderous look. I could not take my eyes off him. He sensed my rage and hatred as he turned and started up to the second landing.

Thinking back to that evening, I am grateful that the door to the outside was on the second landing and was not locked. Reaching that landing, I hesitated only a moment, grasped the handle and stepped out into the fading day.

I headed for home. That night, after my bold walk along the road from the school, I was determined I would never again stay at that school. I continued walking on the side of the road, not bothering to run into the ditch to hide when I met a vehicle.

I surprised Mom when I walked into our kitchen. This time, there was no tongue-lashing as in my first runaway years earlier. It was obvious that something bad had happened. She gently washed and cleansed my face as I related my experience to her.

Despite the circumstances, Mom decided I must return to school the next day. My mind raced as I tried to think of a plan to avoid going back. Finally I told her, "Mom, you can take me back, but I'll run away again and will not come home."

Dad was on the night shift at the paper mill, and they talked in the morning. I don't know what negotiations then took place, but Mom was resolved that I must continue my schooling. She and Dad arranged with the school that I would finish the year as a day student. At lunchtime, I'd leave school as soon as classes were over and walk for half a mile to friends of my Mom and Dad's to eat. I would come home every day after school. Mom's determination about my attending school had not been compromised for the moment.

I returned to school the following year as a resident student with the understanding that my tormentor had been moved away from Fort Alexander. However, this experience and the knowledge that I didn't have to endure residential school stayed with me from that day. I knew that I could leave, even if I had to disappear from my family and community to do so. I carried this attitude into my first year at Assiniboia Residential School on Academy Road in Winnipeg just as I turned 17 years old.

This school was opened in 1958 as an experiment, placing Indian children in a large urban community. It was the first in Manitoba to do so. It offered grades 10–12, as Indian residential schools on reserves in Manitoba offered only up to Grade 9 at that time. I was among its first students that year, all of us being removed from our reserves a hundred or many hundred miles away from Winnipeg.

Immediately at the beginning of my life at Assiniboia Residential School in Winnipeg, I was incredibly taken aback to be given a level of freedom I'd never before experienced at school. That first winter, 1958–59, we were allowed to take snow shovels beyond the school grounds and wander down specific streets in the neighbouring River Heights area, offering to clear snow from sidewalks and driveways. Three blocks from the school, I and two schoolmates encountered a smiling lady who answered our knock on her door. She spoke with a lovely British accent and asked if we were from the "Indian school." She accepted our services and asked if we wanted a drink of cocoa when we finished shovelling.

A curious young girl had appeared behind her mom to see the "Indians at the door" and we shyly acknowledged her with a smile. My mates and I had introduced Indians to a friendly and kind family. (Twenty-four years later, this young girl, Morgan, and I became partners for life.)

Against Mom's wishes, I left school before the end of Grade 11, my second year at Assiniboia. Although I didn't finish school then, I went back 11 years later in Edmonton, in my late 20s, and got my high school equivalency. I went on to get a certificate in civil engineering technology at the Northern Alberta Institute of Technology.

In spite of the burden of dealing with the effects of Indian residential schools, First Nations at that time were beginning to attain their educational goals to some degree, though the Department of Indian Affairs still controlled who could attend post-secondary school. As I'd been accepted at school in another province, Alberta, I was assigned an education counsellor from there. Mr. N. and I met periodically to see how I was doing and determine whether I was able to compete with non-Indians. I had to do a few months' study to satisfy Grade 12 requirements for civil engineering. I graduated with Mr. N.'s son, Ron; he was one of my friends from the graduating class.

Mom and Cliff came to my 1973 graduation. A thousand miles from our reserve, there I was, side by side with sons and daughters of "white ladies." I felt Mom's pride and joy when I hugged her and whispered, *"Megwetch,* Mom." I'll always remember that moment, seeing the tears in her eyes and holding my little girl, Jacqueline, who had watched intently through the long proceedings and was also proud, even at seven years of age. Cliff, in a borrowed suit, sat beside Mom, not wanting to speak for fear that we might detect his emotional state. His hand was warm and tender as he firmly grasped mine.

Paradoxically, I was both proud of my accomplishments and withdrawn and shy because I was 7 to 10 years older than the rest of the class. As my healing progressed, I realized that I'd probably overcome more than most of my classmates. Most of them had finished high school and gone directly into college or university.

Mr. N.'s pride in me was obvious and probably gained him high marks and praise, too. He may well have received a positive performance review and possibly some bonus pay as well. He never thanked me, but his praise sufficed. In a brief encounter following the graduation ceremony, he gave me a $200 bursary and said in a short speech that I'd been one of just over 200 Indian post-secondary graduates in Canada that year. The presentation was a small recognition of my accomplishment. Mr. N. didn't have a clue, though, about how lucky I'd been to succeed given my background. And he didn't see the smile, tears and joy on Mom's face when I accepted the prize. Mom's been gone now since 1994; her greatest gift to me is the memory of that moment.

My daughter Jacqueline graduated almost 20 years later at a much younger age than I did, completing a master's degree in cultural anthropology and realizing a dream by going to work at the Smithsonian Institution in Washington, D.C., and later at the Milwaukee Public Museum.

Most residential school survivors follow a pattern similar to mine. It took time for me to deal with the physical, sexual, mental and spiritual abuse I had endured. Like me, most survivors waited a decade or more before going back to school. Some went back even 15, 20 or 25 years later to study the things that as children they'd dreamed of studying. But Canada lost some great contributions from its First Nations citizens because of the residential school system.

MY LANGUAGE IS OJIBWAY

In my years of self-examination and therapy, I've discovered that confronting my early experiences has corrected some malfunctions in me. Thankfully, one thing that no longer plagues me is a fear of darkness. For about 40 years I was unable to sleep or be in complete darkness. I'd have to have light filtering through a door or a blind. This reaction stemmed from my earliest days at residential school.

Once when we were all in the playroom, I was playing on the floor with several friends, reliving a picture show we'd seen at movie night and using small objects like stones and pieces of wood to act as the cowboys. I was startled when Sister S., the supervisor that day, almost knocked me on my back as she wrapped her powerful, bony arm around mine. I'd inadvertently said something in Ojibway. She'd assumed I was referring to her when a couple of the boys laughed at my comment. She yelled that she'd wash out my mouth with soap but instead dragged me to where she'd been sitting. I was shoved into a closet behind her chair. It was under the stairs leading to the second floor and was used to store brooms and other cleaning materials.

I don't remember how long I was in there, but it seemed like an eternity. I was desperate. I tried to sit up but banged my head on the overhead stairs. I tried to see the light under the door. Hearing the sounds of play outside the closet at least made me feel closer to my classmates. I clenched my eyes to visualize my cousin Dee and me frolicking at Treaty Point. I stretched my legs—which rattled a pail in the closet and then upset it. Sister S. hissed at me to be quiet. At least her crackly voice reassured me that someone was nearby. I sobbed for a while, to no avail. Eventually she let me out. Her first word was "*Tiens!* (Take that!)" followed by a warning not to speak my "savage" language.

That is the experience that for years made it impossible for me to be without some light. Initially my counsellor and I thought my fear had been caused by a predator perhaps having wandered around the dormitory at night. That was true, too, but it was the closet experience that scarred me. I can now sleep in complete darkness.

As a young boy I spoke only Ojibway. I did know certain things in English from hearing them said by others; I remember taking great pleasure in calling one of the big boys, a cousin of mine, a "son of a bitch." I now pray that his mother and mine understood my ignorance at the time and forgave me. I'd probably have left him alone if he hadn't reacted and chased me and growled that his mother wasn't a dog. I didn't know what that meant, but I delighted in the chase and his reaction. He occasionally caught me and slapped the back of my head, without much force. I'd then take off again and yell "son of a bitch" if I knew I could escape. When he started ignoring me, I became bored and stopped taunting him.

Years later, I asked him if he remembered these episodes, and if he wanted to replay the chase without reference to his mother. Being an elder, and wise, he replied, "Go ahead. I'll just watch you," knowing that my knees were as bad as his and that if he did take up the challenge it'd be a contest to see who could better withstand the pain and who could walk the fastest.

My education in English was long and tedious, and the lessons sometimes very surprising. Spending time on our reserve and hearing Ojibway had allowed the priests and others in authority to learn some of our language and sometimes understand the gist of our conversations. The nuns in particular would listen intently when we whispered and talked in Ojibway. They'd pretend not to hear or understand us so as to catch us saying something they didn't like. I thought then that this was one of the reasons we couldn't speak our language. I later learned that they thought it was a language of savages and not created by God.

I remember a time when a nun's ears were on high alert. I think we were in the grade 3 or 4 classroom. One of the good nuns was the teacher we called *Pa-kok-achi-chan*—"baseball nose"—as the tip of her nose looked like a baseball. A characteristic of Ojibway culture is that individuals are often known by prominent features or characteristics and get nicknames because of them. These stick for a lifetime, and although they may sound uncomplimentary, they're personal and accepted without shame except when bestowed with vengeance.

Anyway, I used a new word to describe her. I don't know what consequences I'd have had to endure if the more combative Sister S. had been the target of my smart-aleck remark. I presume I reacted to some order such as "pull up your pants" or "wipe your dirty nose" or "don't you know how to tie your shoelaces yet?" In any case, as the nun walked away I whispered, or so I thought, to a friend, "*Kitchi mungi cheet.*" "Big arse" wasn't very complimentary, but the habits nuns wore were very bulky and made them look huge—perhaps in order to scare us. Some nuns and staff were very sensitive about how they looked, so sometimes their reactions to innocent comments were unwarranted and had serious consequences.

In this instance we were well into our lesson when there was a short, sharp rap on the door. In came Father R., the principal.

He was known as a tough priest who often sat at the back of the church during Mass to hear confessions. Sometimes he'd be sporting a black eye or bruise he was rumoured to have got in a scuffle at a Saturday-night party at a hotel outside our community.

This day he walked boldly into the classroom and asked if I was there. I let the nun answer, and he asked me to raise my hand. He knew I was there, so his barging in and asking for me was intended to terrify me and everyone else. It reminded us that he was the boss and it was unwise to upset him.

I meekly raised a wavering hand and slid down to make myself as inconspicuous as possible. Father R. said, "I want you to come to my office at recess," and walked out. Everyone turned and stared, smiled or smirked at me, because they knew it couldn't be good. It was never good when you were called to the principal's office. Mostly it was when you were in trouble or there was news of some catastrophe in the family.

For the next hour I didn't hear a thing or acknowledge questioning stares. I thought I was going to be sick. Tick, tock, tick, tock—the hammering of the clock grew louder as it wound down toward recess. Perhaps I'd trip and break a leg on the way to the office.

I don't remember the conversation or full punishment. I've still blocked that from my mind, but I know I received some lashes from Father R. for using bad language about our good sisters.

Most priests and nuns used leather straps that the school's farmer had cut from pieces of tractor belts. They were about six inches long and three inches wide, and they hurt!

I remember being terrified that day, crying and also wanting to hurt Father R. somehow. I was sent back to class after I'd searched for the word "arse" in a couple of dictionaries in Father R.'s office. The search was long and tedious and took most of what was left of regular class time. When it came time for dismissal for the day, when we usually had time to play before supper, Father R. reappeared and asked me to stand with him while he spoke to the class. He said that I couldn't find the word in the dictionary and explained that what I'd meant was "ass," not "arse." I was quivering as we stood there. He told everyone that they couldn't leave until I'd completed my punishment for having used a word in a way that Catholics couldn't understand.

The blackboards ran the length of the front wall of the classroom and half the length of the side wall. I wasn't very popular as I began writing "I will never use the word arse again," filling the front and side blackboards. Sister Pa-kok-achi-chan once or twice erased a line when she thought my writing was too big. We almost missed the supper bell. I'd robbed my classmates of one of our favourite times of day. My guilt was enormous. And the fact that I hadn't learned yet to say genuinely "I'm sorry" provoked further hostility in my classmates. The incident didn't teach me respect, but it did make me angry at and distrustful of the priest. I didn't blame the nun for the punishment because what I had called her was what I saw and she still had a *mungi cheet*.

I know now that the stress of incidents like these caused me to stop speaking Ojibway. I also thereafter was never late for anything, having felt so guilty for causing my classmates to miss their play before supper.

In 1984 a federal study predicted that by the year 2000, Canada would have only 3 out of 53 Aboriginal languages remaining. The rest were reported to be endangered or verging on extinction. These languages are unique to Canada and are the main means by which culture, identity and spirituality are articulated, shared and passed on to successive generations. Later it was also reported that one of the Six Nations languages, Tuscarora, was no longer spoken or written in Canada. Yet in 2010, the strength with which Canada's original languages are flourishing highlights the strength, resolve and emerging control of First Nations people in this area.

FRIDAY FRUITS

On Sundays when our parents visited, we sometimes got money from them to buy things from the rectory or to donate to the Pope and other Church leaders. In the rectory, the priests' quarters, there was a small room with glass-fronted dressers and closets full of religious items such as medals, holy water containers, neck scapulas, religious pins and other items that we could buy for ourselves or our families for special days like Christmas, Easter, Mother's Day, Father's Day and even St. Patrick's Day. Classes competed in donating money to help foreign missions in places like Africa.

It always seemed to be Africa, the competition sparked by our seeing a photo of a young, forlorn and dirty child. I wonder how much of our donations actually reached such children. Parents would hand over unhesitatingly whatever money they could spare, and the school took advantage of that generosity. We kids often compared these unfortunate children to some within our midst and to younger siblings at home. Occasionally a student who was the butt of the laughter would tattle and we'd get an earful and be told that we'd taken a step down the ladder to hell and to be sure we went to confession.

At the front of our classrooms was a very noticeable, brightly coloured picture. At the top was God, surrounded by bright yellow and white flashes of sun. At the bottom was a deep red hole in a broken-away piece of land. In the hole were people in obvious distress and pain; they all had gaping mouths and eyes, and flames shooting out of them. Nearby were devils with pitchforks, looking joyful, horns protruding from their red heads and bodies.

The middle of the picture was a depiction of life on Earth. Ladders connected to both scenes, one leading to God and one to the devils. I was scared for a few nights after I first saw this picture, and it was often referred to by our teachers, who encouraged us to give freely to requests for money so that we could ascend the up ladder.

In those years, work was hard to come by, so the money collected from reserve residents came from a lot of hard work, much of it menial. Mom, for example, walked five miles to and from the homes she worked in every day. She did the cleaning, laundry, baking, cooking and whatever else the white ladies required. She was paid only two or three dollars a day. Dad had been unemployed for maybe one day in his life and often worked six days a week—Sunday was never a day to work. When he retired from the Pine Falls paper mill at age 65, after 32 years of working there, he made less than $90 a month as pension.

The coins we got from our parents for Africans and for purchasing little presents occasionally resulted in a little personal profit, intentionally or not. In my case, leftover coins sometimes disappeared into the pockets and hiding places of bigger boys, either stolen or obtained through intimidation. Once I hid coins beside a pole at the baseball diamond, about six inches below ground. I intended to retrieve them when the need arose. Alas, within a week I saw a tractor working on the field and replacing the poles and backstop. I stared in anger and disbelief at what was being done. Later I shuffled around the site to find my coins, to no avail. I thus learned early that money and other material objects have no value if you don't use them. I now use a financial institution and advisor for my savings.

A few children were day students, as I mentioned earlier. One such was a boy named Rodger. I didn't know then that he was related to me. Occasionally a group of us would gather part of our profit from Sunday visits and convince Rodger to buy us a pound of lard. It was delectable and filling and enhanced the taste of hardtack biscuits, which were as hard as mud on roads. Someone later identified them as dog biscuits.

Rodger seemed to enjoy his assignment. I suspect he added varying degrees of inflation to the purchase price of the goods. Parents might wonder why we wanted to know the cost of a pound of lard at the store, but Rodger never had trouble purchasing it. He also bought other small items such as toffee and chocolate bars.

Sometimes a smaller group, perhaps two or three boys, would make a joint purchase of something. I don't remember how long this went on, but I was only part of a partnership once or twice. I heard that someone had got caught transferring some goodies and suffered the consequences. Rodger had been reprimanded and his parents were visited by the principal. From then on, day scholars were watched closely to ensure they did not bring any more goodies to school, and our supply was cut off for good.

I don't remember the school serving any fruit to us other than rhubarb, which I grew to hate and still do, except occasionally in a pie. But I do remember my parents bringing me a bag of fruit each week. Before I was in residential school, I would rummage through grocery bags and boxes every Saturday night when Mom and Dad came home in a taxi or other hired car with the following week's or two weeks' supply of groceries. Bananas and grapes were always my first choice. I was allowed a treat before supper and grew to love them. All through my residential-school life, Mom replenished my fruit supply each Sunday, without fail. She'd put the bag on my lap and I'd eagerly open it and practically shove my whole face into it to smell the apples, oranges, bananas and other fruit. Depending on what was available in the store, sometimes there was exotic fruit such as pears, peaches and grapes.

Knowing Mom's habits and generosity, and knowing that I loved these treats, the nuns would take and count my fruit. I didn't know why and thought perhaps it was to show that they were in charge, or to make it appear that keeping the fruit for me was a favour. Eventually I realized they were rationing it. Almost anything to do with everyday activities was controlled by the nuns, including collecting, distributing and storing anything brought to us from home on our parents' weekly visits.

After counting the fruit, the nun would put the bag in a cupboard 8 to 10 feet up from the floor in our playroom. Every day she climbed a ladder to the cupboard to retrieve a piece of fruit for those of us with a bag up there. I enjoyed the piece at the beginning of the week, but grapes or bananas always seemed to be handed out at the end of the week. After five or six days in a hot cupboard, my favourite treats were almost always spoiled and smelled like the homebrew at Old Gus's house. Sometimes I shared my fruit with other children not as lucky as I was. Even when I thought I was being generous, I sometimes felt guilty. It was usually the end-of-the-week treat I shared.

Sometimes I tried to stash fruit on my body or elsewhere before the count so that I could collect my treasures later. But the nuns somehow knew the exact number of pieces of fruit Mom had brought and would find out where my treasures were. As time went on, I asked Mom to bring an extra banana, apple or other goody and I tried to keep the extras secret.

I resorted to tricks. I tried hiding an apple in the water tank of a toilet, but I lost it because it lodged in the mechanism and caused the toilet to malfunction. The nun suspected me but couldn't prove I was the culprit. Once a snitch told on me. I became very adept, however, at swearing my innocence. I never tried the toilet trick again. A garbage bin seemed to work best, as long as I was the first to go to the bin after the Sunday visits were over and I had volunteered to clean up.

The thrill of putting one over on the nuns was greater than the satisfaction of biting into an apple after retrieving it unde-tected. And my volunteering to clean up often garnered praise the next day from the teacher. My knowing smirk to my friends told them I'd been sneaky and fooled the nuns. Fooling authority became a reprieve from boredom, and defying authority became a way of life when I was an adult. Eventually, my Sunday baskets didn't have bananas and grapes; Mom wondered why I'd come to hate them. Years later, these fruits sometimes made me gag because of memories of the cruel controls at residential school.

Residential school life thus taught us well how to be cunning, deceitful and untrusting. But as I heal, I am learning to trust and to be open. And now I again enjoy peeling and savouring a firm, slightly green banana.

MIND, BODY AND SOUL

During all the economic ventures our family undertook, I don't recall instances of alcohol use except on one occasion. That's when I first heard the phrase *keeshkwaybee*, which means literally "crazy from drink." The phrase stuck with me because it was scary to think of someone nearby being that way. I heard the phrase at a wild-rice camp. Mom was making tea or something after supper. She asked Dad about meeting some people concerning the misbehaviour of a camper, who I now know was intoxicated. All I understood at the time was that someone had been sent home.

Keeshkwaybee became very familiar to me after residential school. That demon alcohol became a friend to most survivors in pre-healing days. Although I never did like the taste of beer, I enjoyed the carefree feeling it gave me and found I could say and do things more easily when drinking. Perhaps more significantly, the idea that I'd be punished for using it was always an enticement and a dare to flaunt authority in my early drinking years. Drinking was my choice, by golly, and I wasn't going to be controlled by anyone. This idea of not succumbing to authority remained with me for most of my life.

In my healing journey, I began to understand that alcohol abuse wasn't a genetic flaw and that not all Indians become alcoholics, as insinuated by some people. It is merely a means of coping with other, bigger problems. This isn't a cop-out, as we can all make choices, but alcohol's effects are cunning and can make a person feel as if he hasn't a care in the world; it's also a great confidence-builder.

Those of us from residential schools were mentally crippled by the experience and clueless about what we were or were supposed to be. Most survivors left school in their teens or early 20s, and most didn't live long. They were trapped at age seven or slightly older in psychological, emotional and spiritual age. For many, it has proved difficult or impossible to recover.

For almost 50 years I was on one terrible ride, but thankfully I've ridden out the tsunami of anger and grief caused by residential school. Looking at old photos from those days I see strong, capable, young Anishinaabe boys who left this world much too early. Anyone who says the system didn't have a negative effect on young Indian children held captive there has never seen or felt the anger and shame that can surface at the most awkward moments.

On my own healing journey, I've learned that the mind creates a deep sense of and belief in one's unworthiness, causing hate, despair, skepticism and cynicism, in the face of long-term abandonment and abuse. I entered residential school a loved and loving child, but changed under the care of black-robed strangers. The attack on my mind from the first day at school caused a progression of bad effects. Unhealthy perceptions and feelings cause the whole body to malfunction by releasing doses of negative chemicals into the system. But in healing circles, it's the mind that is the driving force.

The soul becomes a desperate hiding place for the good within us and battles constantly with a dark presence that tries to shove aside all that is good in us and overwhelm positive memories and beliefs. The bad effects of our early school years surface every day of our lives, affecting how we live. It is when we finally remember, and confront our hurts, that we begin to heal. We aren't "survivors," as most former residential school students like to call ourselves, but "victors." Although we were brought to an unnatural state that devastated most of us for most of our lives, we've emerged later in life and done what we needed to do to live worthwhile and happy lives—at least, some of us have.

Almost all former students suffered from their experience. Many died early and tragically. Those of us who didn't have survived with much help from our families and a dedicated and extraordinary health care system. It's true that we hobble through middle age with more drugs, more crutches and wheelchairs, and sometimes fewer limbs than the average Canadian. We may be a long way from attaining the average lifespan, but our healing is obvious in that we are living longer than expected.

Yet federal and provincial government documents assess the "disease burden" of First Nations people as much higher than that of the general population. Governments keep statistics about premature deaths and epidemics among First Nation populations without exploring why they occur. I think that the after-effects of residential school are the real causes of ill health among many First Nations people.

For example, poor dental care at my school resulted for most of us in a lifetime of poor dental health. Untreated abscesses in teeth and gums cause infection. Constant infection and temporary healing through antibiotics scar arterial walls. Lucky people like me were diagnosed and received surgery. But the treatment can also be incapacitating; we've all experienced deterioration in quality of life. Reduced strength and endurance have limited our mobility and ability to benefit from exercise and sports. Most people, including me, have had to leave the workplace prematurely. And for many, the fear of dentists and doctors and lack of faith in them has led to ignorance and avoidance of potential help and services.

At my school, as in most residential schools, we were seen by a dentist once a year. In our case, it was Nurse D. She appeared every September or October and again in late spring. She stayed for two or three weeks and treated half of the children on each visit. I don't know if she was actually a dentist or not. We called her Nurse D. because that's what she was called in the announcement about her visits. She arrived with dental tools, mostly pliers and drills. She had dirty blond hair and, although she was not large and most likely was loved by her husband and children, she struck fear into even the big boys.

She must have tried to save teeth, as her drill was always whirling. If you were unfortunate enough to be next in line, waiting outside her room, you could hear it and wanted to run away. She didn't use painkillers to dull pain. At least once or twice during your "fixing and cleaning," as she called it, she would touch a nerve with the drill. Women say that childbirth is the ultimate in painful experiences, but I think having nerve endings in your teeth touched by a drill or squirted with cold water probably loses by only a nose, or a tooth.

I remember screaming and almost jumping from the chair, and then getting slapped on the back of the head or having my ears pulled and being called a baby. Later, I was more macho and didn't want people in the waiting room to think I was a sissy, so I tried to hide my reaction, but I still shed inadvertent tears and experienced excruciating pain.

These visits were some of the most hated times of the year, and Nurse D.'s coming caused enormous stress and illness. When informed that you were to be "fixed" on a visit by Nurse D., a common response was "I think I went last time." Alas, it was to no avail.

Many diseases and other health problems First Nations suffer today stem from intergenerational attitudes and what survivors inadvertently pass on to their children, sometimes with the misguided intent to make life better and less painful for them. Parental guilt over losing children to residential schools resulted in widespread resolve by parents to compensate for not fighting enough to keep us home. When we went home in the summers, we'd be showered with practically anything we wanted if it could be afforded, including a lot of candy, pop and other unhealthy snacks.

Diets at school were another problem. It's apparent that we were to appear to be well fed. Our diets, I suspect, were intended to fatten us up through a high intake of fat and cheap protein. The Church realized huge savings in its food budgets that way. Expenditures must have been far less than the huge transfer payments received from the federal government for feeding and supporting students in residential schools. The Church also hired a few people from the reserve to work at the school. They were often paid less than minimum wage; some people suspected that the Church practised creative bookkeeping and reported higher wages to the government, which reimbursed it for such expenses.

Our food had an overabundance of unhealthy fats, starchy food, carbohydrates, sugar and salt. A typical school breakfast was porridge. It was served almost every day. I vividly remember the bowl being about 10 inches in diameter and one or two inches deep, something like the oversized pie plates my mom had. The porridge sat in a blob in the centre of the bowl. I'd seen concrete being laid; the porridge always reminded me of a shovelful of concrete dropped on a slab of wood flooring.

Sometimes the porridge was warm and liquid-like, but mostly it was a cold blob. It was filling but sometimes made you gag, depending on how much salt had been added. It was once rumoured that saltpetre was also added to it. Like most students, I grew to dislike it intensely. I didn't eat porridge for 20 years after leaving school.

At school, Friday was a day of abstinence, so breakfast was a plate of milk, made from powder. A slice of bread soaked up the milk. We sprinkled our allotments of sugar on top of the bread. The school breadmaker, Mrs. B., probably noticed that on Fridays she had to bake extra loaves, as many grew little feet and disappeared. I didn't think she ever saw us as we snuck into her domain to steal bread; I think now that she deliberately busied herself away from the doorway so as not to see.

Lard and grease were staples. Lard was a delicacy, cut into one-and-a-half-inch squares about half an inch thick. I often wondered who created those squares. I thought perhaps it was the girls. I learned later that it was people like Mrs. B. or someone else from the reserve. They scooped out lard from pails into a half-inch-deep layer in square tins and stored them in the cold pantry overnight. In the morning, workers removed the pans and ran knives through the lard to create squares while it was still cold.

On special occasions, generally related to holy days in the Church calendar, we were treated to real margarine. This was also served when our parents were visiting, such as on Mother's or Father's Day. I remember some yellow powder being sprinkled on top of our cubes of white margarine. I never did discover its composition, but I took great pleasure in mashing it in so that the margarine actually looked like butter. Two or three times a week we discovered solidified pieces of bacon and pork grease instead of lard. That happened when kitchen staff had collected enough discarded cooking grease to feed to all of us. The congealed fat would be a treat of sorts and a welcome break from our usual lard allotment. How often we got it depended on how many bacon-and-egg breakfasts or pork-roast dinners the priests, nuns and brothers had consumed.

We could only smell the aroma of such food wafting from our keepers' dining rooms, which were across the hall from our own. For years after leaving school, I gorged almost every day on bacon, sausage, ham, bologna and eggs. I'd cut long slices into my toast and insert tracks of butter into them, and I routinely laid a piece of bread or bannock in the pan where I'd just fried bacon and let it soak up the grease, unaware of the health risks associated with eating this treat. I'd acquired a taste for a high-fat, low-nutrient diet, which later contributed to my clogged arteries and need for open-heart surgery.

Now I eat oatmeal that is hot, smooth and sprinkled with raisins and some firm banana slices or blueberries and a pinch of golden brown sugar. It's again a staple of my diet and I enjoy it two or three times a week.

First Nations people are now taking back control of their healing and lifestyles, so the health of our people will improve immensely. Although statistics indicate still that First Nations people will die five or more years younger than non-First Nations, I foresee a time when the average lifespan for our people will meet or maybe exceed the Canadian average, as was true for early generations of my ancestors. It was only once the residential school system was well entrenched that life expectancy plunged. I expect to live beyond the average life expectancy for males in Canada, despite my health problems and former self-destructive behaviours. The strength and health I inherited, my willingness to learn to be healthy, the support of my family despite my persistence in hanging on to some residential school habits, and an improved health care system all contribute to my expectations.

KILLING THE INDIAN
IN THE CHILD

Mrs. B., the breadmaker, was one of a few of our loved ones who worked at the school. She also assisted the nuns and other workers in the kitchen, in the laundry and with such duties as knitting and sewing. Restricted from direct contact with us, these caring few acknowledged us from a distance, without fanfare, but such instances brightened our days and we craved even a glimpse of them.

Mrs. B. was well respected by children of all ages. In my era, two or three of her children were also at the school. That must have been a joy as well as a deep sorrow for them. Having their mother go home each day after work without them must have had devastating effects. I shudder to think what my attitude and feelings might have been if it had been my immediate family member who was there and he or she had been disallowed to show feelings and affection. I can't imagine a heavier burden than if my mother had worked at the school five days a week, yet been withheld from me.

Sometimes Mrs. B.'s children sought her out, hoping to catch a glimpse of her before she left. It was terrible for them if they missed even seeing her from a distance before she left. On the other hand, the anticipation of seeing her the next day must have been wonderful.

Years later, when a few survivors began to talk about their experiences, I remembered how I'd viewed relatives who worked for the school and the church: I'd slowly become indifferent to them. Eventually they were neither band members nor relatives. They were just workers at the school. Even children with mothers or fathers working at the school sometimes came to see them as "just workers" or servants. Some lost all understanding that the far-off woman in the kitchen was their mother. Some were ashamed that one or both parents worked there, and some saw them as a part of the residential school regime somehow. Yet, if you weren't immediate family, you could see these people as a connection to home and the reserve, and as friends of your family, these servants of the church were a welcome distraction.

The last day of June was the beginning of our summer holidays, which lasted until the first week of September. Initially, that was our only release from the school. By our third or fourth year we were also given a week at Christmas.

For the first two or three years I distrusted Mom and Dad when I got home, and would stay away from them and my siblings, sometimes by myself, sometimes with my cousins. I'd spend a great deal of time at the river's edge and at its swimming areas, wandering along the bush trails with my slingshot and stopping to pick berries along the way. These excursions took me back to my younger days and my years of freedom before school. Mom and Dad always knew where I was; Kookum, Mishoom, my siblings or other relatives knew where to find me. By the end of the first two or three days, I'd have forgotten my mistrust and would greet Mom and Dad enthusiastically when they returned from work. Reflecting on these initial reactions, I see that I had learned to become aloof in my mistrust. This would be one of the typical behaviours that I and other survivors bestowed on people we love.

In our early years at school, we savoured the safety and freedom of our homes and became oblivious to having to return to school in September. After a few days back at home, we reverted to enjoying the closeness of family, the freedom to speak Ojibway and our relationship with the environment. We enjoyed these short holidays, not realizing they were meant to wean us off the way of life at home and on the reserve.

Our response to the holidays became more subdued the longer we were at school. The dull realization that in no time we'd have to come back to school lessened the joy of anticipated freedom in June. Even now, thinking about summer holidays and going home at the end of June makes me giddy, and then suddenly I remember that those times were short-lived and in some ways made our incarceration even worse.

This ambivalence ensured that we became more and more subdued as we got older. I began to see the unadulterated joy of young boys and wonder if they understood that they'd be back in September. As a young child free from school and at home for a while, I had resolved to do whatever I could to prolong the experience. But predictably, I became used to school life as time went on and related more with the priests and nuns who had become so familiar. I got so used to being in school that my closeness to and contact with my family became less and less important; the separation meant that our lives and interests had become disconnected.

Some residential school survivors still believe and vigorously defend their belief that nothing ever happened to them there. I disagree. The mind adjusts to any situation and attempts to attain a state of happiness and safety. When we refuse or are unable to achieve a sense of calm, our lives follow a path of turmoil and self-destruction. We suffer the consequences, manifested by our health and other physical realities. It's incredible how well our minds protect us to ensure our mental health and safety.

Survivors of Indian residential schools in Canada became victims of Stockholm Syndrome long before it was a familiar term around the world. The misguided sense that some of our keepers were kind and good was based on single and rare acts of kindness and support. In most cases, we came to see our keepers as saviours and protectors from hunger, isolation and abandonment. We watched parents and family leaving the school on that first day and blamed them for leaving us. We blamed ourselves for being left behind, abandoned because we weren't wanted or had been bad. We blamed ourselves for still being hungry, isolated and alone.

As young children, easily manipulated, we created new connections and rapidly bonded with some of our captors. Being malleable and wanting kindness and love, we slowly came to believe that there was kindness in those we were around every day and attached ourselves to those who looked after us.

Looking back on my years at school, I remember fondly some nuns, priests and others who I think were truly there in the belief that they could help us adjust to a foreign way of life. I believed at the time that they didn't want to change us so much as teach us what we needed to succeed. I'd hate to think that those few priests and nuns who were kind were hoodwinked into practising a method of manipulation that resulted in the Stockholm Syndrome.

They emphasized that we wouldn't see our parents until the next Sunday, though we'd never before been away from home for even a night. They pounded into our little minds that our families couldn't look after us as well as the school could. This was the biggest hoax and tragedy bestowed on Indian people and their children in Canada by residential schools. The removal and separation of young children from their families and the manipulation of their minds to hate their Indianness was the biggest abuse and the most common method used to kill the Indian in us.

In some cases, the actual caring and benevolence by Church people was genuine. It was nevertheless very effective in manipulating the minds of young First Nations children. I remember the emotions and desperation of that first day of school incarceration in my first direct contact with the Church and priests. I still experience overwhelming feelings of horror, anger, hate and abandonment when I think of that day. Father R. allowed me to see my parents walk out the door and down the sidewalk and recruited my cousins to restrain me. Clem and Marcel used force to hold me. I blamed them then, and Mom and Dad. Although I eventually understood it was not their fault that I had to be left at school, the idea that it was their doing had been effectively planted in my mind. The blame had been shifted from the priest and the Church to my family members.

Over the years, I came to appreciate my cousins' genuine caring and concern. I remembered that they stayed with me through supper and the early evening. This gave rise to a brotherly love that remained with me until their deaths. I miss them still.

I also recalled later that Father R. approached me after supper that first evening as I sat in front of what was to be my locker for the coming year. Even though Clem and Marcel were there to console me and had hardly left me alone, I was deeply affected by the afternoon's activities and felt terribly alone and lost. I experienced strong panic when the priest sat down beside me. Although my knowledge of English was minimal and I only understood a word here and there, his voice and tone were very soft, and it sounded as if he cared about me. I thought he might protect me and make sure I was okay in this strange environment. Perhaps he'd help me get home somehow. After my forceful separation from Mom and Dad, his behaviour served as a first step to replace that abandonment by transferring my trust to him.

Father R. participated in a wide array of sports; his macho style endeared him to all the boys at the school. He was very competitive and this enthusiasm often pitted "his" boys against Indian boys and men on the reserve. Although we also often encountered his strap, head slaps, kicks and other physical attacks, most boys looked up to him.

Another man who had the support and following of a large number of boys was Brother M. He was somewhat like Father R. in that he sometimes appeared to have a deep disregard for the nuns and their rules. He sometimes changed those rules. For example, he ordered the nuns and kitchen personnel to allow a school hockey or baseball team to have supper while fully dressed for the upcoming evening competition in Pine Falls or Powerview. Such games were proud moments when we showed off to the other kids by parading into the refectory in our hockey gear. Brother M. would speak loudly to the nuns, who were either cooking or supervising, yelling that he wanted "his boys" ready to leave and not having to waste time getting ready after supper.

I remember him once grabbing a white lay farm worker by the scruff of his coveralls, shaking him and yelling at him because he hadn't finished cleaning and preparing a field so it was ready for "his boys'" baseball game. There were other such instances; he was an example of how children were conditioned to feel love and respect toward their captors.

One Saturday afternoon, after Brother M. had been transferred elsewhere, we were on our respective playgrounds, boys on one side and girls on the other. Various activities were under way; there was a baseball game on the boys' side. Suddenly a fielder lost focus as he stared at something down the road. He hollered, "Brother M.! Brother M.!" and pointed at a figure approaching the church. Immediately a group of boys, four or five at first, then more than a dozen, ran to meet him.

As they crossed the girls' playground and the rectory road and thundered into the churchyard, there stood an awestruck lone figure contemplating taking flight up the road or refuge inside the church to get away from this scruffy crowd. Maude, an old friend to many on the reserve, was visibly taken aback and somewhat shaken by the unexpected crowd of young boys around him. Although he was well known and liked by almost everyone on the reserve, he wasn't Brother M.

Maude was obviously embarrassed and a disappointment to the boys, who immediately scampered back to the school grounds. For years, poor Maude endured jokes and laughter about this incident, and light-hearted comments like "you'll never be a brother" and "the priests have to save your soul first." The incident did provide some comic relief to the kids at school—even more to those who didn't run toward him that day.

Like Father R., Brother M. wasn't without a reputation for a quick temper and quick hands and fists, though most of us were fast enough to make sure his boots didn't connect with our most vulnerable parts. His violent and volatile temper was well known, and although he sometimes verbally belittled us as Indian people, our claim to being "real" Indians had been lessened by church sermons, classroom teaching and comments, the school environment, cowboy-and-Indian movies, condescending treatment of reserve residents, and the idea constantly instilled in us that we were now better than our reserve families and community. The job of getting rid of the Indian in us was being well done by the Church, government and teachers.

STRUGGLING TO SUCCEED

M om and Dad instilled in me a work ethic that stayed with me all my life. As a young boy, before I entered residential school, I cut and chopped wood and brought it inside and stacked it. I had to ensure that the pile would last for two or three days. I know I would have done this prior to leaving for residential school because it was a fall and winter responsibility, from before the snow in fall to its melting in late spring. I also helped my grandparents and other relatives get ready for Christmas by stocking their woodpiles.

Another chore I remember vividly was ensuring that our water supply was adequate. Every day, sometimes twice, sometimes three or more times, I went to the river with two five-gallon aluminum pails and fetched drinking, washing and cleaning water. In the winter, my tools included an axe, an iron chipping pole and a piece of rope that was attached to an older, banged-up pail. I used this pail to clean out the freshly opened waterhole and then draw water from the hole and fill the other pails. We often joked and laughed in the family about the length of my arms. For years I thought my arms were longer than other people's because of all the heavy pails of water I'd carried from the river, and I still attribute my muscular legs to all that water-carrying.

Most reserve families owned a boat and motor and a team of horses for general transportation and, more important, for fishing, hunting near the river and lake, and hauling firewood and cordwood for the mill. When I was six and seven, I was occasionally allowed to lead and walk George and Bess, our two huge workhorses, to the waterhole for a drink. Dad would be nearby to help if I needed it.

Most mornings my routine included a foray with my slingshot into the bush by the river to check my snares. I'd gather the rabbits and any ptarmigan that had been caught or wandered into the path of my slingshot. I felt important providing a delicious meal for my family.

I presume that my entering residential school caused hardship for Mom and Dad and my relatives, as they'd have had to replace me in the jobs I'd done. And I missed the rewards for doing the work (bannock and sweetened tea, mostly, and sometimes cookies and pie) and the closeness with my family and relatives.

At first, I recall, I eagerly anticipated coming home from school for Christmas and resuming my role. Later, probably in my fourth year, I'd come home at Easter, too. But, as I've noted, once I went to residential school, I became an outsider and a non-contributor to family life. I could never again on a daily, full-time basis help maintain or contribute to my own family, or help relatives or elders. I'm fortunate that at least the memories of these activities remain with me and are so very real and clear.

I thus entered residential school with a work ethic. I carried it with me despite the turmoil I felt, and performed my duties well. Sometimes kind and encouraging words inspired me to try to do more to please the priests, brothers and nuns. But at school, my tasks were only labour-intensive activities and not intended to improve my skills or knowledge. Jobs normally done by school employees, like piling wood in the furnace room for hours at a time in the winter and on cold days, ensuring that the furnaces were full of fresh wood, and sweeping and washing dormitories, playrooms and washrooms, were all part of our "education" at school.

To feed the children and staff, the school had workers plant the huge fields near the property with potatoes, corn and other vegetables. These were stored in a root cellar on the riverbank when they were ready, and our chore was to haul the harvest into the cellar and retrieve vegetables from it during the year.

In my third or fourth year, I was one of the boys to help in the fall harvest. The boys in grades 4 to 8 were pulled out of classes for this, and although the nuns and teachers thought the priests, brothers and supervisors didn't need so many boys to pick vegetables, the principal ruled that they all could miss classes to work in the fields.

I'd seen this happen while I was in lower grades and thought the bigger boys were lucky to be out of school and in the open fields. I would watch with envy as they wandered out with their bags, pails, hoes and rakes to begin their day-long chores. When they came back to the refectory for the noon meal (called "dinner"), we all watched as these "working men" joined us little boys and stood at their designated places at the long tables. Once, as grace was being said by a priest, I envisioned myself standing on that very spot with rumpled overalls, well-worn boots and rough, calloused hands, taking a break from an important chore.

When I finally was one of the big boys, I still thought the job important. After dinner we'd strut around the boys' playroom, then wash up and use the facilities. After perhaps a half-hour, the priest would holler at us and we'd line up to return to the fields. The routine of bending, kneeling and lifting could last for a week or two. The monotony was broken for the boys selected each day to haul and carry vegetables from the fields to the school and the root cellar.

The priests and supervisors occasionally gave us a break and a treat by taking us down to the granite point behind the church. There we could strip down to our underwear and jump into the river. Most of us gladly did so, as it was a relief to feel the cool Winnipeg River, but a few didn't. One day, there was an incident that changed everything. We'd finished work and gone to the river as usual. Students who didn't want to swim were sitting on the rock washing their feet and splashing themselves.

Father R. must have been annoyed for some reason with Rene, who was a mischievous and rambunctious boy. Rene was one of the boys who didn't want to go into the river. When Father R. ordered him to "get out there," Rene still refused! The priest then pointed at some bigger boys and ordered them to help Rene into the water. They literally threw him in. As soon as he hit the water he thrashed and floundered about, yelling for help, and disappeared. It was obvious he couldn't swim, so a couple of boys jumped in and dragged him out after he'd disappeared a second time. Unfortunately, this incident ended the liberty that most boys had looked forward to. Rene was more subdued after this incident.

Other jobs I remember from when I was a little boy at school were scraping and hauling refuse from the big red barn that housed the horses and cattle the school owned. Although a white farmer and his family were responsible for milking the cows, he trained an employee from the reserve to do the actual milking and passed on that knowledge to the boys cleaning the barn. It was our chore also to haul the huge cans of milk to the kitchen.

I also remember mending clothes in a room on the second floor of an attached building between the big boys' side and the main building. The nuns had found a way to salvage and repair our clothes, and had given us some basic instruction in patching, darning and knitting. Mending clothes had formerly been a daily chore for the girls, but they couldn't keep up. So three or four times a week the littlest boys would be taken to this big room filled with boxes and boxes of old socks and clothes and taught how to repair them. As we mended pants, socks and shirts, Lone Ranger stories would be on the radio. We learned to enjoy and admire him. Tonto, his sidekick, came to be known as only an Indian who had no significant role except to follow the Lone Ranger around. We understood Tonto's name for the Lone Ranger, *Kemo Sabe*, to mean what it does in Ojibway: "taking a sneaky peek." We believed Tonto was Ojibway, one of us, and that he used this name because his boss always wore a mask.

On my summer holidays, I worked at various jobs, and because of my relationship with my family my paycheques went directly to Mom to help with family expenses. So I wouldn't feel I was working for nothing, she gave me an allowance that I could spend however I wanted to.

I did a wide range of work in those summers, and because I so enjoyed being free, some jobs lasted less than three or four weeks. A cousin and I once spent four or five weeks painting the outside of the Sagkeeng Seminary for way less than minimum wage, for example.

I pride myself on having had the courage and determination at that time to tell Father P., head of the seminary and also assistant at school, that I didn't need help addressing my personal hygiene. My cousin and I brought this issue into the open so that we could support each other. I specifically asked him, "Did he try to wash your *pinjik* (crotch)?" He said, *"Nee meeg ann a* (I will fight him) if he tries." We were beginning to look like big boys, and this "hygiene" practice would never again be "required."

As I got older, summer jobs became more stressful as I became more aware that some managers had superior attitudes toward Indian people. I believed then that we were in fact less capable of doing what white people could do, as the nuns and priests had taught us that we could not ever have the jobs of bosses. My confidence plummeted as I was exposed to more and more of these superior attitudes.

When I walked away from Assiniboia Indian Residential School in Winnipeg when I was 18, I went home to the reserve for two months. I lived with Mom and Dad and resumed my preschool duties. My newfound freedom and lifestyle obviously needed financing if I was to live away from home, so I began to think about how to find real jobs. The mill then was operating at full capacity and needed wood for its newsprint and other paper products. My cousin Howard and I decided to go in together to deliver pulpwood to the mill. I'd learned the skills involved in producing pulpwood when I worked with Dad and Uncle J.B., as well as with Cliff and Leon.

Working on the reserve was comfortable and enjoyable, but the wood had to be delivered to Pine Falls. Visits there were somewhat stressful because they required meeting with white employees to determine the price we'd get for our wood. I'd never been involved in delivering pulpwood to the mill, where the producer/cutter could deliver and "negotiate" a price that was different from the mill's basic price. This so-called negotiation was never a process in which we could justify our product or discuss price.

To me, "negotiating" merely meant having mill representatives and scalers point out the flaws in our product (too small; the core of the pulpwood is a bit dry; butt ends are too jagged, or a couple of inches too long). These "flaws" meant that we had a lesser product and so got a reduced price. The negotiation was one-sided, but we thought that if the wood wasn't satisfactory, the scalers would actually reject the load and we'd be stuck with it.

The arbitrary penalties imposed by mill representatives usually meant we received $11 per cord instead of the usual $14. A cord consisted of four-foot lengths of pine or spruce trees piled four feet high and eight feet long. On a good day Howard and I could manage a cord. In those years we had only axes and bucksaws, not chainsaws. As young entrepreneurs, Howard and I

Me on the steps of Fort Alexander Indian Residential School, Manitoba, in 1950 (my third year there). My mother had this image made into a Christmas greeting card that year. She must have seen family photos on Christmas cards in the homes of the white ladies she worked for.

PREVIOUS PAGE Rear view of the school in 1947 (top). The boys' playroom was on the basement level, and classrooms were on the main floor. The boys slept in the second-storey dorm, seen at the far left. The bottom photo shows the dormitory side of the school in 1960. **Archives of Manitoba, Fort Alexander 1 (N14381)**

Aerial view of the mission and school, circa 1948. Families could reunite briefly on Sundays outside the church. The school and grounds are behind the church; farther back is the farm where older students worked. Parallel to the shoreline, adjacent to the cemetery, is the dirt track I walked with Mom and Dad the day they brought me to the school.

LEFT Dad at age 16 (left); Grandpa Schall, seated in centre; and Dad's eldest brother, Alexander, in 1916. Grandpa Schall was fiercely independent, and he passed this trait on to his sons.

TOP RIGHT Mom's grandfather, Niizhotay, with two sled dogs and a trapping prize, in the wilds between Fort Alexander and Manigotagan, *circa* 1920. Mom's father, a trapper like Niizhotay, left her in the care of nuns after her mother died.

BOTTOM Fort Alexander school staff and students, *circa* 1915. When my dad's brother Tony was reprimanded, Grandpa Schall had quite a confrontation with Father G. (seated, centre left).

TOP Grandma Therese and Grandpa Schall with my cousin Jackie, between Fontaine Point and Treaty Point on Fort Alexander reserve. Jack was the son of my dad's sister Ellen Jane. Therese mentored Mom in being a wife and mother, as Mom had no role models to teach her these skills.

BOTTOM Classes at Fort Alexander, *circa* 1926. On the girls' side, Mom is second from the right in the second row from the back. Mrs. B., the school's breadmaker when I was there, is third from the left in that row. Dad's brother Albert is at far right in the second row, and Father G. is in the centre.

TOP Four of Dad's eight brothers (left to right): Gabriel, brother-in-law Monroe Gordon with son Jack, J.B., Albert and Charlie, in the late 1930s. Dad and J.B. frequently worked together on various economic ventures, sometimes with one or two of their other brothers. I have fond memories of these family adventures.

BOTTOM Uncle J.B., his wife, Agnes, Mom, Dad and my brother Leon at age 19. Leon excelled at cadet activities in residential school and enlisted in Princess Patricia's Canadian Light Infantry at age 18. The day after this photograph was taken, he shipped out to Korea.

OPPOSITE PAGE The Fontaine family, *circa* 1935. My brother Leon and sister Marie are in front, Grandpa Schall and Grandma Therese are behind them, and my parents, George A. and Margaret, are at the back. My oldest brother, Cliff, was already away at residential school.

LEFT Father P. and some of his students in the late 1940s.

MIDDLE My class in a study room, *circa* 1949. I'm in the second row, visible between the two boys in the front row.

BOTTOM Some of the nuns at Fort Alexander Indian Residential School, *circa* 1950. I and others remember Sister Mary of the Incarnation, second from left in the front row, for her kindness.

TOP My classmates and me in about 1949. I'm the little guy at the front in the solid sweater. At the far left is my cousin Marcel, who was enlisted to take me from my parents on my first day of school. The principal, Father R., wears the black robe and cross that made him look so scary to me that day.

MIDDLE Parents of Fort Alexander students, *circa* 1950s. Chief Paul Courchene is in centre front; my mom and dad are directly to his right.

BOTTOM The Fort Alexander midget hockey team enjoying victory after its first Indian tournament in 1956. I am at the far right in the back row. Brother B. is at front right. An encounter with him later that year altered my life dramatically.

TOP Me in the white-sleeved jacket, my close friend William, one of the over-age players on the Fort Alexander hockey team who helped secure our win, and our now deceased friend Luke at right. The photo was taken a few days after our victory in the All-Indian Residential School tournament in Brandon, Manitoba, in 1958.

LEFT Me in 1963, in Rossland, British Columbia, to play senior hockey with the Rossland Warriors. This was a chance for me to get away from life as an Indian in Manitoba. My aptitude for the game eventually led me to a life-changing opportunity.

Philip Fontaine   Ted Fontaine   Luke Chubb

PREVIOUS PAGE, BOTTOM Assiniboia Residential School in Winnipeg, 1958–1959, where I found a level of freedom I'd not had in my previous 10 years of school. Insets of cousin Phil, me and our friend Luke, from the student portraits from that year.

TOP Dad and his girls: My sisters Marjory and Marie, Mom, my sister Shirley and Dad, *circa* 1961.

BOTTOM Dad with Marie's daughter, Lori, *circa* 1966. Dad had just retired from the Pine Falls paper mill. His retirement was short-lived; he passed away six years later.

TOP LEFT A night of great joy and celebration after graduating as civil engineering technologists in 1973. Paul and I are seated in front; behind us are Cam, Ron and Robert. At far left, partially hidden, is Howie.

TOP RIGHT A snapshot I took of some of the boys on my crew during a mineral exploration trip in the Northwest Territories, 1970. My years in exploration in the NWT proved to be a critical turning point in building my self-esteem and professional capabilities.

BOTTOM My older siblings Marie and Cliff, me and Mom, on the day after my dad's funeral in 1972.

TOP On a plane with my daughter, Jacqueline, in 1971, flying home from the Northwest Territories to visit Mom and Dad. I was early in my healing journey at this time. My girl, with her beaming smile, was and is the joy of my life.

MIDDLE Jacqueline and I on a holiday at the Hoover Dam in the United States, circa 1976.

BOTTOM Completing the circle, with Jacqueline at the opening of an exhibit she planned for the Milwaukee Public Museum, circa 1995, while completing her master's degree in cultural anthropology.

TOP Mom, *circa* 1955, checking out her garden after work, with the smile I cherish.

BOTTOM Auntie Margaret, me and Uncle Albert, *circa* 2000. Uncle Albert became a mentor and close friend after my return to Fort Alexander in 1977.

TOP LEFT My dear friend and cousin Allan (Chubby), *circa* 1974. It was Chubby who initiated the frank discussions of our experiences in residential school. His untimely death in 1997 devastated me, yet propelled me forward in my healing. The photo was taken by Allan's daughter, Dixie.

TOP RIGHT Angus Merrick, friend, elder and advisor, *circa* 1990. During my time with the Assembly of Manitoba Chiefs, Angus visited me at least once a week. He taught me to confront the abuses I experienced at residential schools and helped me learn that I could deal with them.

BOTTOM Elder Barney (Joseph) Williams, a critical support to me on my healing path. Barney sat with me for more than eight hours as I went before an adjudicator and government lawyer dealing with my abuse claims in 2008.

TOP In June 2010, I visited Fort Alexander (now called Sagkeeng). The school and its outbuildings have been bulldozed, but a few remnants linger. A portion of a chimney and a stray piece of barbed-wire fence are evocative reminders of my years there.

BOTTOM My wife, Morgan, and I in 2010. We first met in 1959, when I was a student at Assiniboia Residential School. Many years later our paths crossed again, and we became life partners. **Leona McIntyre photo**

were ecstatic to make $11 a cord, which we received in crisp one- and two-dollar bills. Thinking about it now, this arrangement must have been lucrative for mill representatives, as they probably received more than $14 a cord to pay producers like us. At least we didn't have to find a place to cash a cheque.

I don't recall ever having a chance to discuss the "flaws" in the pulpwood. The mill representatives were supreme and the residential school had taught us well. We didn't argue with white people. Although bush work and its freedoms were enjoyable in themselves, my uneasiness and feelings of intimidation and shame escalated and became part of who I was in my dealings with white workers at the mill. These men, like others in my work experiences later, knew I was an Indian from the reserve, and they made sure I felt inferior to them.

I wanted to tell them that they were a bunch of crooks. I learned to take comfort in booze. Howard and I would wait outside the local hotel after we'd sold our wood and pay someone to buy a case of beer for us. My bad feelings of being less capable or not smart enough to take jobs that were normally done by white folk were eased by booze. I could make the feelings disappear. Those guys at the mill or anywhere else couldn't make me work for them. I didn't have to deal with them—I could move to a different job. I could go someplace where they wouldn't know about my Indian heritage or think I was less than them.

Eventually I contacted the Department of Indian Affairs, and the Indian agent convinced me to take an electrician's pre-apprentice course in Winnipeg. I didn't know that it was a practice of Indian agents at that time to ensure that any reserve member schooled beyond the reserve education system be helped to find a way of life away from the reserve. I remember the Indian agent assuring me, "If you want to leave Fort Alexander, I will help you all that I can." Although I thought I was being helped, I see now that I was actually being pushed away from the reserve as part of the policy of assimilation.

For the next couple of years I was employed by a number of firms, beginning with an elevator company and culminating in work at a larger electrical firm. During my apprenticeship there, through no fault of my own, I had a major jobsite accident and spent three or four days in the Winnipeg General Hospital. For years thereafter, I was fearful of doing simple electrical work like installing a plug or a light fixture, and I suffered headaches. During these two and a half years after school, I apprenticed to five electrical firms in all and never made more than 98 cents an hour. The attitudes I encountered, and the lack of training and mentoring, would cause me to abandon my job for days at a time. Of course, such actions always led to my being fired or given a lay-off notice.

My employment record for the next few years is a blur. I drifted from job to job, doing everything from electrical apprenticing to hauling dirt for a new golf course to laying forms and concrete on Winnipeg city streets. I worked as a salesman and as a driller. I cleared brush for a forest slasher and was a contractor for forest clearing. I was a newsprint wrapper at a paper mill and a sewer-line pipe-layer. I held various jobs across Manitoba and in other provinces. I found that people would pay me for almost anything I could do. It was thus easy to find work with enough pay to support myself and my lifestyle.

At one point during this period, when I was 24, I got married and moved back to Fort Alexander. I got a job at the paper mill and became a father to my precious bundle of joy Jacqueline. Being a new father motivated me to try to find some stability in my work. I had always been taught that I was to take care of my family, and I was determined to do so. Shortly after Jacqueline's birth, I relocated to Winnipeg to find a better job and began learning the skills of legal surveying. I worked in this discipline for about a year and a half.

Then one day, a friend suggested I contact a hockey team he'd heard was recruiting players for its senior team. He'd given them my name, so they expected me to contact them. Since I'd been playing a bit with a local team, I thought I could still play competitively. So, in my mid- to late 20s, after speaking with the team rep and without any guarantees, I boarded a Greyhound bus and headed to Peace River, Alberta. Not expecting much beyond not having to go back to my old job, I made the team and became a Peace River Stampeder in the North Peace Hockey League. After I'd secured the position, my family joined me there.

After a few months of hockey and working in an electrical firm to supplement my salary, I fell into the familiar rut of feeling guilty and inferior. After-game episodes of drinking were becoming the norm. Fortunately, a higher spirit stepped into my path through an old friend and drinking buddy. Gil, a Frenchman I'd met in Manitoba, lived and worked in Pine Point in the Northwest Territories, which was about 300 miles north of where I was. He had heard I was playing hockey in Peace River and had driven for about eight hours to see a couple of weekend doubleheaders.

On his second visit, Gil told me he'd been asked to approach me about moving to Pine Point to put together a team to compete in a northern hockey league the following fall. Apparently Cominco's Pine Point mine was willing to pay for my move and put me on its payroll to subsidize my salary as a playing coach. This possibility became more real with each phone conversation with Cominco. I had no knowledge, no confidence or any idea how to coach a senior hockey team, but it sounded like a good opportunity.

The Stampeders coach, Cecil, and the team had been good to me in Peace River. Cec was also the sheriff there and had taken me into his home, as if he knew how ignorant I was about life. I'd lived with him and his family for almost a month, until I made the hockey team. After I became a full-fledged member, Cec arranged for me to rent an apartment and for a local electrical company to hire me. I deliberated whether or not I could abandon the team. I knew the Stampeders were high in the league standings, so they could afford to deal some players to other teams. I also knew that a teammate had recently gone to another team, the Grimshaw Huskies, and that he was happy there.

Conveniently and suddenly, my abandonment question was resolved when Cec pulled me aside during a practice and said he wanted to talk to me after the weekend series about another team in the league, which had expressed interest in me. He wanted me to consider being traded to that team. My dilemma was solved. I didn't have to abandon the team and I didn't have to just sneak out of town and leave, as the team didn't need me! I told Cec that night that I'd be leaving. I then phoned Gil and asked him to arrange for my arrival in Pine Point.

Although I did skate with the prospective team in my new community, I never made a formal commitment to it. Pine Point has a population of over 6,000 people, many with Aboriginal connections, and I was comfortable there. Instead of being engaged in hockey, though, I threw myself into my new job at the mine. It allowed me to work outdoors almost exclusively and to pursue my interest in engineering. I became more comfortable working at a site where the workforce was less judgmental about my Indian status, and I stayed in Pine Point for two years, the longest I'd been with one employer up to that point.

In those two years I became head of an exploration crew and had unquestioned authority. Mentoring from the geological staff strengthened my capabilities. The feelings of inadequacy pounded into me from age seven were challenged by my supervisors' confidence in me. Eric, as head geologist, had agreed with George, the head technologist, that the duties of exploration crew chief could be assumed by someone who knew electrical matters and survey principles. Thus, at age 27, my self-perception and confidence took an upward swing, and I knew I could do the job. I also acquired some capacity in legal surveying, which later enhanced my status in mineral exploration. My experience at the Cominco mine, and the personnel there, turned the tide for me. My attitude improved, and I started to write about my experiences at residential school and to pray.

Despite my job satisfaction and love of mining exploration, I decided I had to return to school for post-secondary credentials if I was to go further. So I moved to Edmonton and enrolled in the civil engineering technology program at the Northern Alberta Institute of Technology. During summer breaks and as my confidence and self-perception deepened, I experienced the joy and satisfaction of working for and with my people again. I became regional coordinator of the federal Indian summer employment program in Edmonton, and soon after graduating from NAIT in 1973 I was offered employment in Ottawa, an opportunity that solidified my interest in improving the lot of First Nations people.

Although it was a satisfying period, the attitudes and perceptions I'd attained at residential school hadn't prepared me for the true mindset of the federal government and its bureaucracy. From early attempts at self-government to the present day, First Nations people have had many dreams and expectations die because of the prevailing belief that Indian people are incapable of governing themselves. Paternalism and condescension toward our people have been the standard attitudes of federal and provincial governments and their agencies and organizations responsible for health, education, child welfare, police and social services.

The final and most significant phase of my working life, from 1975 until my retirement in 2000, was being employed by my people. After the year I spent in Ottawa training in land management, I became regional land administrator for Indian lands in the Northwest Territories (NWT). I was stationed in Edmonton, but the work took me to various Indian communities in the NWT. Working every second week up north meant that I was unable to establish real roots. Eventually I found a job in Winnipeg with Parks Canada, coordinating employment and business opportunities in the six national parks and six national historic sites in the Prairie region.

Less than a year later, the chief of the Fort Alexander band, my friend and cousin Phil Fontaine, negotiated a secondment with the federal government that allowed me to be on loan to the band and retain my government employee status. And in less than a year after that, Phil left the chieftainship. I stayed with the band but cancelled my secondment. The next year I worked as an advisor and economic development officer for my community. In the fall of 1978, I acceded to having my name put forward for the upcoming council election and subsequently was elected chief.

In the 1970s, Phil and others had established an elders' recreation centre on the reserve that gave community elders a place to meet. During my administration, we did some more creative planning and established a senior citizens' home. It was a day of celebration and pride when senior federal bureaucrats told us that the home was the first to be established on an Indian reserve in Canada.

No longer would our senior citizens be forced to move to an assisted-living facility away from their home and come back later only to be buried in their community cemetery. It had been a common lament that when our seniors left, they returned in a box. The joy and satisfaction of helping to develop our community whetted my appetite for continuing to work for our people. I'd bypassed the hurdles created by residential school and was comfortable in what I was doing.

My last 11 years in the workforce were in the service of the Assembly of Manitoba Chiefs, going from a lands administration position to becoming executive director of the Assembly, then negotiator of the national employment equity agreements and then, ironically, to the position of advisor on Indian residential school issues. In this last role, I represented the Assembly's views and negotiated with the federal government on actions directed at resolving issues raised by residential school survivors in Manitoba and across the country. My journey through the haze, the growing up and the struggles of my early years had brought me to the satisfaction of helping and taking pride in our people's survival. I was happy to have survived what I'd lost 50 years earlier.

Looking back now at the 50 or so jobs I've had, I see my work history in distinct phases that reflect my state of mind during and after residential school. In my early preschool life, the training I got from my immediate family and other relatives taught me to see work as fun and as a way of helping my family and others. I learned then not to be scared of work.

In the first years after I left school, I was never more than a few days without work, thanks to the strong work ethic instilled in me when I was young. But none of the jobs lasted long. My school experience and perception of my Indianness had given rise to a disturbing pattern of my quitting or being fired. I basically kept running to where I wasn't known as an Indian and starting over.

Each time I started a new job, I tackled it with enthusiasm and vigour. But eventually, or sometimes even on the first day, a superior or co-worker would express some difficulty about my being Indian. For example, a newspaper reported a court decision to bar an intoxicated Indian person from the community after a weekend brawl. The following Monday morning, a supervisor at the encyclopedia warehouse where I worked said to me, "We don't want trouble here," implying that because I was an Indian too, I would behave the same way as the person in the article. Within a week, I was told I'd been laid off, that there wasn't enough work to keep me on.

Some mornings I'd wake up with an incredible hangover and try to remember where I'd been. I would vaguely recall arguing at a bar with people I worked with. Sometimes I didn't even return to my workplace and just moved on. Eventually, I began to analyze why my record of employment was so horrendous. Employers were appalled when I finally stopped hiding the long list of places I'd worked at and the reasons I'd left. I'd been subconsciously challenging employers to hire me in spite of my heritage and then fire me because of it.

My confidence started to grow as I gained training and experience, especially when I was leading a rough and tough crew in mining and exploration. That was a chance to expand my knowledge and learn management and leadership skills. Sadly, my career was hindered by my late start, which shortened my involvement in First Nations struggles and programming, where my abilities could be used to help my own community.

But in examining my working life during my healing journey, I was pleasantly surprised at the continuity I had had for over 50 years. I was proud that I'd been independent and not had time without work. I lost years and years when I could have been pursuing a comfortable and financially stress-free life, but the jobs I had *did* support me and my family and allowed us to have the amenities we needed. And although it's been difficult to become comfortable enough with myself to stay long at a job, I'm thankful to have experienced what I have.

Most survivors have travelled similar roads. The Roman Catholic Church and the federal government had been so thorough in dismantling my self-perception of my race that any allusion to it caused upheaval in my life. I went from job to job trying to keep ahead of society knowing who I was. I turned to alcohol to enter the part of my mind that gave me peace and strength. During those periods of reprieve and hangover, I began to write about and analyze why I was malfunctioning, why my heritage caused such hate and discrimination, and why I reacted the way I did.

I began to understand how the feelings instilled in me at residential school had led to my horrendous employment record. In many workplaces, I got the clear message that I was expected to be incapable, lazy or have to be assigned a co-worker because I wouldn't understand what I had to do. For example, after completing the electrician's pre-apprentice course at the Manitoba Institute of Technology in Winnipeg, I began work with an electrical firm. When I suggested to a supervisor a way to do a particular task, he retorted in front of our boss, "Oh, it can talk, too!"

I also vividly recall my Grade 9 teacher, Mr. B., standing in front of the class and saying, "You people will never drive a new car because you will never be able to afford one through your jobs doing labour work." I thought then that perhaps I'd never achieve anything worthwhile in the workplace. Mr. B. later became superintendent of education for the Department of Indian Affairs in Ottawa. I phoned him one night many years later in a moment of bravado and, in an alcohol-induced drawl, asked him, "Mr. B., do you know what I am driving?" Little did he know that my white truck was brand new. I was beginning to think differently about my capabilities and to view the attitudes of white society as adversarial and bigoted.

I developed a deep sense of suspicion and wariness, always looking for ulterior motives lurking beneath the surface of day-to-day encounters and activities. I remember an Indian hockey tournament in the late 1950s for midget-aged residential school students in Manitoba. Fort Alexander Residential School won the inaugural tournament in Winnipeg despite our being told by everyone that we didn't stand a chance. We barely lost the second-year tournament to a much bigger and better team. I later learned that some over-age kids were on the winning team. The third-year tournament was held in Brandon. We won handily again and brought the trophy back to Fort Alexander.

Although the organizers cancelled subsequent tournaments, they gave no reason for doing so. What we knew as members of the Fort Alexander team was that three of our teammates were ineligible to play in that Brandon tournament. Our principal (Father B.) and our coaches (white supervisors) had included three good over-age players on our team under the names of eligible but much less talented students. The priests and supervisors had learned well from the previous year's experience, and intended to ensure that Fort Alexander was again the tournament champion.

The reserve hired a bus for community residents to come and watch the tournament. Boys from the higher grades were on the bus, and the younger students whose names were on the team roster were also allowed to come and watch the game. While in the foyer waiting for his drink, Joe Guy, one of those younger students not on the team but whose name was on the roster, heard Father B. hollering, "Come on, Joe Guy!" from the players' box. The player he was calling to, Bill, who was nearly 18 and thus ineligible by two years to be in the tournament, had just scored a goal for our team.

Father B. had lied when submitting our roster. Joe Guy's name was on the roster, but Bill was actually playing. And despite knowing some community members would realize what he'd done, he brazenly called out the name of the player who'd lost his place to an older player. We wondered if all schools did the same thing.

Father B. thus taught us to lie to accomplish what we wanted, and to be untruthful about what we accomplished in our work. I recall once telling a work supervisor that I'd finished a task because it meant I'd be free for the rest of the day. I'd actually installed only 6 of 12 plugs, figuring I'd do the rest the next day. It was easy to lie because a priest could do it, too.

The biggest problem to overcome as an adult worker was my need to be free after having been confined during my childhood. I was dreadfully affected by being confined to any particular area. Even after just a few days on a job, I would feel choked and restricted. Knowing I'd leave the job soon felt good, like getting out of school at the end of June.

So it was with much satisfaction but also some trepidation about not having completed my service that I retired in the early 2000s. Now I volunteer, knowing I can provide some help and support and that some good may come for those less fortunate. I always remember my less than fortunate time in school. But I no longer need the praise and recognition for helping others that I craved back then. As a friend once said, I like to fly under the radar. I also don't need to get awards or enhance my resume.

Understanding the reality of being an Indian has been the most difficult and cumbersome task I've faced in my 60 years. It was masterfully drilled into me that I was a "heathen savage," incapable of being white or doing what the white man could do. I've had to come to terms with the realization that Canada has tried hard to rid the land of its First Peoples, and has contravened the laws of humanity. That reality surfaces periodically still, although bigotry and ignorance have become easier to handle and now only come up with less informed individuals.

It's unfortunate that at the long shadow of my life I'm only beginning to treasure my worthiness and uniqueness, and take joy and comfort in my Indian status. I have so little time to do so fully, but at least I've come to appreciate my own culture.

CHUBBY

An unlikely catalyst in my confronting my residential school experiences was my dear friend and older cousin Allan. He was the second-youngest of a large family of more than a dozen children, all of them older than me. Their mother was Dad's sister Sophie. Although Dad and Sophie were very close and the families visited as much as possible, transportation in the late 1940s and early 1950s was an adventure, even for short distances. I remember well the visiting done with Mom and Dad before I entered school and, most vividly, during the summer holidays. It allowed me to get to know our uncles, aunts and cousins more closely. Sophie and her husband, Ambrose—we knew him as Mis-Kus (Red)—lived approximately two miles from us, past the residential school.

Allan was more than three years older than me, and as a kid I thought of him as a big macho guy I only saw at family functions, visits, weddings or funerals. His playfulness and work ethic were always evident, and I looked up to him as someone I wanted to emulate. I was actually a little afraid of Allan and stayed close to my family when he was nearby. When I entered residential school he'd already been there for two or three years, so we had no relationship there.

We saw each other the odd time during holidays. I remember another cousin and me going with Allan to an afternoon movie in Pine Falls during a summer holiday. I don't recall much about the day except that we wandered around after the movie and heard hollering, laughing and splashing at the swimming pool, which was close to the theatre. We peered through the wire fence there and saw kids enjoying the cool water.

After much debating about what these white kids would do if we took a swim, the blazing sun made our decision. We ripped off our clothes, left them piled by the fence and leapt into the water. An adult soon came over and summoned us to the pool's edge. I thought, "Oh-oh, this pool is not for Indians." Sure enough, we were told we couldn't be there. Allan argued. Finally the attendant stated bluntly that we couldn't be in the pool because we didn't have swimming trunks. Our undershorts were too revealing. Although I had felt safe being with my big cousin, this was an instance of our not understanding what was proper or not proper around white people.

Another memory I have of Allan is him chasing me around a snowbank at his house during the Christmas holiday, and burying my head in the snow after he'd had enough of my teasing. He'd grown up a lot faster than most boys on the reserve, as had his siblings, because of his mountainous father, Ambrose, who had strict expectations for his children. It's not my place to tell Allan's story, but in later years we talked about what it was like growing up in that family.

Ambrose, being a trucking and construction contractor, taught all his sons the nature of his business, including operating trucks and construction equipment. He pulled Allan out of school early to work in the family trucking business, which is why I didn't see him for years. His dad convinced Church authorities that Allan was old enough and was needed at home. From his dad, Allan learned how to run tractors, bulldozers, transport trucks and other heavy equipment. He drove all over Manitoba. Later, while he was still a young man and I was elsewhere in the country, he became great friends with Dad, and eventually our bond as cousins and friends was renewed and cemented.

We started calling each other Chubb because when we first met after not seeing each other for eight years or so, he (and presumably I) appeared a little chubby. That encounter broke the ice. This mutual name evolved in meaning over the years and was an expression of closeness and brotherly love. Allan would also greet other relatives and friends with nicknames in a lighthearted way, because it made it easier for him to start talking about serious issues like residential schools. However, he didn't do so consistently and the nicknames never quite meant what ours did to us.

When I moved back to Manitoba in the late 1970s, Chubb and I caught up with each other again. I had been chief of the Sagkeeng (Fort Alexander) band for almost a year. Chubb recognized my need for a break and a return to the basics of life, so he asked me to join him and his nephew in gathering wild rice. Thinking I'd enjoy renewing my knowledge about that activity, I agreed. I didn't know that Chubb had arranged for a charter plane to fly us to a remote lake northeast of Sagkeeng, where I would be completely isolated from my work and duties as chief for a whole week. Chubb and his nephew would stay for 12 days. When we landed at Octopus Lake with all our paraphernalia, including a canoe attached to the plane's landing floats, I was excited.

The first day was mostly spent setting up the campsite. The next day we harvested wild rice until sunset and we couldn't see to pick anymore. We sat around the campfire with our evening meal, made small talk, reviewed our day over tea and then went to bed. On subsequent days, we had our evening meal and then lay on the rocks, watching the sky and counting the satellites making their way across it. One night I was startled and dumbfounded by Allan saying, "I wonder if Father P.'s actions could be seen if someone was looking down at us from one of those."

There was an awkward silence. I couldn't imagine that little priest taking advantage of my macho friend the way he'd done with the small boys. Then I realized that Chubb had been small once just like me, so would have had similar experiences. His simple comment allowed us to talk about the ménage and tell each other what had happened at school. By the end of the week, we had remembered the names of priests, nuns and brothers and had categorized their places on a scale of mean and abusive behaviours.

Besides suffering the probing hands of Father P. and others, Chubb told me he'd once been knocked around by Brother M. and kicked "in the rear" because the brother believed he was neglecting his chores; he'd gone to the toilet without telling his supervisor. Chubb thought the school authorities figured it was okay to be physical with him because his dad was so strict that he wouldn't care.

When we reminisced about our younger days and our residential school days, it made me feel a bit relieved to know that some things didn't happen only to me. I had never before talked about my experiences to the extent I did with Chubb. The joking and casual mention of what had happened began to evolve into more serious and therapeutic talks. These talks made me realize that I needed to deal with what had happened to me and how it had affected my life. During my years of being locked up at the school, I had thought my family, as well as others in the community, did not realize or understand that this was not natural. Why would they not allow us to live at home and still go to school, like the white kids in town did? Chubb had started to think about these things, too, and about the unnaturalness of residential schools, long before our wild-rice adventure.

After that rice-picking trip, the name Chubb or Chubby forever replaced Allan and Ted. My formal confrontation with what had happened after my seventh birthday became a life-long journey. A few months after this trip I went to see my first counsellor to start dealing seriously with my memories. After my sobering talks with Chubb, I marvelled at the idea that I could lead a community as big and vibrant as Sagkeeng.

Over time, Chubb and I dug deeper into comparisons of our experiences. Questions of healing or compensation weren't even remote ideas then. We were just letting it out and were comfortable talking about how we felt about being in that school, that it was not right and that it was a bad experience. When you live your whole life with the idea that you experienced something unnatural, and if you don't have an outlet or place to dump the garbage, you begin to wonder if it happened at all. I'm thankful that I found Chubb again. Otherwise my life may have ended abruptly in some disastrous way or I may never have begun the work toward healing.

From that time at Octopus Lake and on, we provided a mutual outlet for each other, small as it was and although verbal communication was never our strongest attribute. Our conversations brought us closer together, but it was years before either of us could bring up the topic with others, even in our own families. It was another 14 or 15 years before the residential school experience became a hot issue in Canada and attracted the attention of the public and the media.

It was our cousin Phil, who had recently been elected Grand Chief of Manitoba and was getting attention in the media, who shocked a young audience and a reporter in 1990 by saying he'd been sexually abused at the Fort Alexander Indian Residential School. All the rumours, innuendo and hidden shame of former students were suddenly out in the open.

I remember Allan saying, "You know, Chubb, I get very perplexed at the idea that our parents would send us to a place like that when everything we needed to know and learn was available anywhere and we were just as smart as anyone else and probably smarter than most of those people who came to teach us." (English wasn't our first language, and having re-learned Ojibway quite well by then, this and other conversations were all in Ojibway; I'm paraphrasing in English as accurately as I can.)

One of Chubb's all-time peeves was government people talking to Indian people as if we were children and having the attitude that they could say anything that suited them and we would believe them. He scoffed at the idea of their thinking they were saying something useful. He believed that government authorities and long-winded, trivial conversations and/or orders from them could be worked around or ignored. I smile when I think about his voice and tone when he expressed himself in this way.

I still find that as First Nations people we struggle with dialogue and discussion, even within our own families. This is a characteristic that might be inherent in all First Nations in both Canada and the United States. Chubb's philosophy was that if something important was going to be said, someone would say it eventually.

I often heard him use the Ojibway phrase *mungi too nay* ("big mouth") to describe a government official or opinionated person at a community council meeting. Sometimes, in my cockiness and wanting to be recognized at functions or meetings, I too have said something aggressively, whether it made sense or not, then caught myself with a self-admonishing "Boy, *ni mungi too nay!* (Boy, do I have a big mouth!)" And then I'd remember Chubb, and his down-to-earth sense and wisdom. It's unfortunate that his star didn't begin to shine brightly until he began to shed the garbage left by his residential school experience.

He was a simple man but also very complex in nature. His way of dealing with his residential school experience and the healing path he utilized would have been a model for what could be done through holistic healing. Although he learned to express his feelings more deeply and openly than anyone I know in our family on Dad's side, he had difficulty expressing love for others. Often a quietness would come over him and he'd gnaw and bite off little pieces of skin from his knuckles and finger joints and be lost in himself. You could see in his eyes that some memory was playing in his mind. I'd sit and stare at him, and Chubb would be completely oblivious until he came out of his trance and exclaimed, "*Yok-i-nane?* (What is it?)" I'd answer, "*Ah Pizan-a-bin,*" an expression that means something like "Oh, be quiet" or "Oh, forget about it." Not until he was close to death did he actually use the word "love," and the closest for me was when he'd call me his little Chubby brother and ask if I needed anything—not as an empty, polite offer, but as a genuine expression of caring and wanting to do something for me. I used to suffer in silence on the numerous occasions when he insisted on buying me lunch or dinner at a greasy spoon. I didn't argue because it was his treat and he was doing something for me. It's incredible that it took more than 10 years from our second encounter as adults to come to the comfortable relationship we had at that point.

I spent the evening with Chubb at Assiniboia Downs racetrack in Winnipeg on a Wednesday night in 1997, enjoying the ponies and a light snack. Throughout the evening Chubb experienced blurred vision, weakness and exhaustion, and he wasn't his usual jovial self. He left before the races were half over. We arranged to meet again on Father's Day, Sunday. He was to bring his sons, his brother Henry and Henry's sons. "I'll see you Sunday around noon, Chubb" were the last words he said to me. My cousin and friend died of a massive heart attack two days later, walking up the bank from the Winnipeg River to his home.

The phone call late Friday afternoon buckled my knees and took my breath away. The talks we'd had and his sudden death strengthened and crystallized my resolve to work on the issue of residential schools and what I'd experienced in my years at the Fort Alexander school. Perhaps Chubb left me in order to give me time to accept and assess the experience with understanding and less anger. In spite of his leaving me when we had just opened the door to discuss this issue, his departure caused me to delve into the issue more deeply, to understand and to expedite what I needed to do for my healing.

He missed out on nine provincial judges' recognizing that what he'd experienced in five years at residential school was unnatural. The judges approved an agreement between the federal government and residential school survivors. Chubb's early death also meant that he couldn't benefit from the proceeds of the subsequent class action lawsuit, which culminated in a national settlement agreement.

Other people at the graveyard at Fort Alexander have probably wondered why I talk to myself when I'm visiting there. While I pray at the markers for Mom and Dad, my brothers, sister and others, I actually carry on a one-sided conversation with Chubb and bring him up to date on my healing journey.

FROM DACHAU TO NEWFOUNDLAND TO FORT ALEXANDER

As I sit here in the protection of my own home, I ponder and review what I've done and what I've written about these last 30 to 35 years. Almost every day has made me wonder about, appreciate and understand my life, and realize that although we are all unique, we are not alone in what we endure. No matter how much hurt, difficulty and misunderstanding we face, there's always someone who has endured something more catastrophic.

I visited Munich, Germany, and the Dachau concentration camp in 1983. As I toured the exhibits, I couldn't help but remember Fort Alexander Indian Residential School and see the similarities between it and where I was, particularly the seven-foot-high fence topped by barbed wire turned 45 degrees inward. Self-pity and anger soon evaporated, however, as I slowly viewed the photos and descriptions of each bunkhouse, dormitory, mess hall, washroom and shower stall. I can still see the people in these photos, the sunken eyes, the pot bellies, the protruding ribs, the spindly, skinny arms and legs, the matted hair and the pleading, despairing look of people confined by war and an evil dictatorship. I could not imagine the devastation and anguish caused by this atrocity of human history, and my own experience at Indian residential school seemed very minute. Nevertheless, as different as the scenarios are, there was something in the eyes of the people in the photos that was familiar; I'd seen it in the eyes of residential school survivors.

I've met former classmates who astonished me by how dramatically they had changed since I'd last seen them. But despite having acquired more muscular arms and legs, neater and longer hair and well-padded ribs, their eyes still looked haunted. I've been taught through my culture that by looking into the eyes of a person you can see the hurts and disappointments hidden within. Most residential school survivors avoid direct eye contact. The blame that's mostly turned inward has caused shame. We don't want anyone to see what's happened.

In 1920, Duncan Campbell Scott, head of the Department of Indian Affairs, directed that all Native children between the ages of 7 and 15 were to attend Indian residential schools. He stated before the House of Commons, "I want to get rid of the Indian problem... Our objective is to continue until there is not a single

Indian in Canada that has not been absorbed into the body politic and there is no Indian question, and no Indian Department, that this is the whole object of this Bill [to establish the residential school system]."

In implementing the intent of the treaties with Indian people—that being to grab the land in order to get its resources and get rid of Indian claims—Scott had free rein to apply his racism and hatred of Indian people to his policy of extermination, using it to integrate Indian people through schools. Scott, who not only rose through government ranks through opportunity but to the highest level in Indian Affairs, understood well why treaties had been implemented. His opinions and views about Indians reflected those of most politicians in his day. Getting rid of Indians meant extinguishing their languages and culture. A critical step was to take control of the children and make them ashamed of who they were.

With the blessing of the government, Scott implemented his residential school policy. It was to be applied through the churches, under the guise of educating young Indian children. The process was accelerated by terrible living conditions in the schools, where infectious diseases, starvation and abuse caused the deaths of nearly half the children who attended them. The death toll in the 1920s and 1930s was estimated at 50,000.

In school we learned to be ashamed of and hate being Indian. We cheered for cowboys as they heroically won great battles against Indians. Indians were portrayed as savages standing in the way of progress, whose only pastime was massacring white people developing the land and resources. Although genocide has often been denied in Canada, history shows that soon after the appearance of Columbus in the Americas around 1500, the practice of hunting and killing Indian people began.

In the early 1800s, Shawnanditht, known as the "Last of the Beothuk," formed a bond with William Cormack, who wanted to preserve the history of one of Canada's indigenous peoples because he was deeply disturbed and appalled by the actions of a "civilized people" against the Beothuk nation. Cormack, a writer and researcher, was born in 1796 in Scotland and died in Canada in 1868. He spent half of his life studying the Beothuk in what is now Newfoundland. He criss-crossed the island with Beothuk friends, trying to help them, and was frustrated and concerned that the treatment of these people by European immigrants was inhuman. The Beothuk nation was well established in the interior of Newfoundland, but at different seasons they travelled to the coast. They'd been making these trips for thousands of years before Europeans arrived. People spent days and weeks harvesting fish, seals and other mammals and birds.

As the immigrants moved onto the island they had "discovered," they decided that the Beothuk were cutting into what they thought should be their resources. The strangers attacked the Beothuk's traditional food supply, cutting off the salmon's migration routes to the interior. This food supply soon disappeared. Missionaries who followed the European immigrants Christianized the Beothuk without any outcry from anyone.

The Beothuk were no match for the immigrants, missionaries and their weapons. Sometimes they were simply massacred for sport. Despite some concern from settlers elsewhere in Canada, the Beothuk ultimately were exterminated. Thankfully the sport of massacring Indian people stopped at Newfoundland, but Canada lost a vital link to its history when the Beothuk disappeared.

The Indian residential school system was a new way to get rid of the Indian, and, for the Church, a way to claim souls for their various religious orders, thereby expanding their influence and increasing their wealth. Although some of the Church's agents and workers became true teachers and mentors, they could not change the true intent and hidden policies of the Indian residential school system. And yet, despite its own genocidal policy, the Canadian government recognized too late the strength of Indian pride and resolve. The 1951 Indian Act, the 1960 granting of voting rights and the bold 1969 attempt to legislate assimilation were all failed attempts to "get rid of the Indian." They failed because residential school survivors have confronted and tried to repair the damage of that system in particular.

In 2007, as part of *The Beaver* magazine's "Worst Canadians" poll, a panel of historians assembled by Canada's National History Society (publisher of *The Beaver*) named Duncan Campbell Scott one of the worst Canadians of all time in recognition of his actions to "get rid of the Indian problem."

APOLOGIES

For the few survivors who accepted Prime Minister Stephen Harper's apology in the House of Commons on June 11, 2008, I hope and pray that it helps in their healing journey. Even most of the Canadians who questioned the validity and sincerity of that event admit that it validated the historical reality of the Canadian government's having tried to extinguish Indians in Canada. The apology doesn't take away the memory, pain or indignity—or affect my healing—but the words will live forever as part of Canadian history. They acknowledge that my experience was real, that great hurt did happen and that society was robbed of the potential of its first citizens.

All those years after my own experience, of being told that my race and status were less than those of other Canadians, that I'd never be able to do what any "normal" non-Indian Canadian could, I was engaged in an internal battle. But a spark within me, fanned by my early years at home, kept me alive, telling me that I was just as good even though my subconscious always convinced me I was inadequate and led me to try to prove that.

In rare cases in my past, I'd had a chance to say I was sorry to whoever had depended on me and I'd harmed. These apologies never changed a situation, however. My intentions were always good, but I never tried to demonstrate that I'd make things right or better. But my apologies did make *me* feel better and gave me a false sense of freedom from the consequences of my wrongdoing.

In my years of dealing with residential school syndrome, and remembering the people who ran those schools, I've tried to forgive their meanness and abuse. I hadn't encountered the possibility of pardon until one day at The Forks, a favourite gathering place in Winnipeg. The issue of residential schools was a hot topic. Some churches had genuinely become quite concerned about what the schools had done to Indians in Canada. Discussion with the United Church had led to its apologizing to the Indian people of Canada.

On that rainy October day in 1991, Indian chiefs and survivors, each with a representative of that church between them, stood in a circle with their hands locked in the traditional show of friendship. As the much-anticipated event got underway, church officials launched into their apology. As they said "and on behalf of the United Church of Canada, we..." church bells directly across the river began to toll. Everything stopped, and around the circle there was a feeling of divine presence. The irony is that the bells were at St. Boniface Basilica, a Roman Catholic institution, and were tolling for the United Church's apology.

At that moment I realized that no apology could make me feel better, and I decided that I didn't need one. The moment did make me feel better about the Church itself, but watching politicians congratulating United Church officials just reinforced my belief that apologies wouldn't help *me* feel better. It wasn't an apology to the survivors; it was a way of making people in the United Church feel better. Only later in my healing journey did I understand that although I didn't need an apology, I had begun the process of forgiveness myself.

Healing is not easy, and it never ends. Although Indian residential school was my life for 12 years, I was fortunate to have been part of the family of Schall and Therese Fontaine, and blessed to have had such loving grandparents and parents up to the age of seven. The strong family values and teachings I received as a child were not taken away from me, and they sustained me through my years at school and beyond. As a child at school, I lay awake at night remembering and reliving in my mind the joys of my preschool family life. As a young adult trying to find my place in the world, I was able to surface from the self-destructive aftereffects of residential school because of those values and teachings.

In later years and now, I often bring myself back to the trusting child, a child who cherishes those relationships that are the foundation of my life.

When I became a father at age 24, I imagined how I would feel if my child were taken away from me at age seven. I knew that I would do anything to protect her, to keep her safe, to pass on to her the gifts of family strength, trust and love. I did my best, as did her mother, also a product of the Indian residential school system. Yet as individuals, and as a young couple, we were living with the barriers of mistrust and dysfunction from our residential school experiences. Our daughter, Jacqueline, endured these barriers. As a young child, she experienced the effects of our behaviours, lifestyles and problems. Although we both loved and supported her, she practically grew up on her own.

My relationship with my girl was founded on a strong love but was held together by only a thin thread during my darkest years of dealing with the grief and chaos of my residential school experiences. As I began my healing, I saw that she had gone beyond the age of seven—the age at which I remained emotionally and psychologically—and had attained a maturity that I was only beginning to discover in myself. My relationship with her mother did not survive the tragedy that was playing out in each of our lives; however, we have each gone on to find ourselves and our places in the world.

Jacqueline was a loving child, in spite of the psychological and emotional instability in our home. She matured into a loving young woman, independent and successful in her own right, perhaps more in spite of us than because of us. She has learned to accept and to move on with her life. In forgiving, she has demonstrated both grace and generosity of spirit. Today, as from the day she was born, she is the treasure in my life. Our family unit is strong with the loving support of her dedicated husband, Ron, and their two boys, Sage and Hudson.

I first laid eyes on Morgan, the woman with whom I now share my life, in 1959, during the last year of my residential school life at Assiniboia School. It was a fleeting moment—a connection I do not believe is coincidence, but rather a moment of grace that would play out its destiny over time. Some 21 years later, our paths crossed again under professional circumstances, and we eventually became partners. Unknowingly, we climbed on the healing train together. I am sure that jumping off would have been the easiest thing for her to do through those difficult early years. We have now been partners for 28 years and were married in 1989.

In my eyes, she has been unbelievable. In our life together, she has experienced my many short and long absences, periods of relapse and recovery, and agonizing periods of silence punctuated by verbal confrontations as I faced down myself.

My wife has supported my healing journey, learning about my experiences only in my darkest moments when I could speak of or write about them. In trying to express them, I was usually overwhelmed with pain. It would take a long time for me to force the words out. My frustration was so extreme that nothing could calm me. Following these episodes, I would be even more pensive, as well as apologetic.

Morgan has probed and searched for me in the middle of the night to see if I have returned safely home, mirroring inadvertently the behaviour of my young daughter in her years of living with me. As did Jacqueline, my wife has had to fight with her fear, wondering if I have ended up, as so many of my classmates have, dead in a vehicle, drowned or lying frozen somewhere. Many nights, as I have fought off predators in my nightmares, she has carefully and gingerly awakened me, staying clear of my thrashing arms and fists. Then she has sat quietly with me, helping me confront the threads of the nightmares.

As I have learned to speak about my experiences, it nevertheless pains me to share them with Morgan. It must be horrific for her to listen to them and imagine the situations. The pictures are vivid and lasting in her mind, as in mine. My emotions are overwhelming, the damage and pain crushing. She tells me that she understands my behaviours and reactions much more now as my healing progresses. I have seen her crying over the little boy who was so hurt, the boy she sees in me. Her tears hurt me the most.

I have learned that dark memories of the past affect every aspect of my behaviours and reactions to everyday situations.

Recognizing patterns, Jacqueline, Ron and Morgan have sometimes been able to talk about these reactions and, together, come to an understanding of their origins. They have found support and understanding through their love for me and for each other. Sometimes they have shared these conversations with me, but they have been careful not to add to the burden that I carry with me every day and night of my life.

My wife has loved me through my healing journey and beyond. By encouraging me to recall and to talk about my experiences, she helps me find inside the little boy who is full of joy and contentment. She also reflects for me the husband she sees, a man filled with love and life's wisdom. Through her, my family has been expanded to include my wife's father, Robert, her brother and sister-in-law, Alan and Nancy, loving cousins, aunts, uncles, nieces and nephews. I am blessed that these family members complete the circle for me and enrich the life that I now enjoy.

In my young life, I was known as Theodore. As an adult, I was abbreviated to Ted. To bring forth the child within, I am Theodore again, although sometimes my wife calls me Taffy. We try every day to realize the full potential of our love and commitment to each other and to our family. We believe that the Creator brought us together for a reason and that we have not fulfilled that destiny yet, but we're working on it, one day at a time.

"COME IN, TCI-GA"

I turn the handle, open the door and slowly step into the room. I am almost overcome with panic. My eyes can't stop darting around various parts of the room and I feel a deep stab of fear. I almost turn around and walk back out. This is eerily similar to what I experienced when I was a seven- or eight-year-old boy and heard Father P. directing me in a commanding, low whisper, "Come in, *tci-ga* (little boy)." But this is not the day of my ménage.

This is the day of my hearing, the long-awaited opportunity to tell representatives of the Government of Canada about my experience in residential schools. I've had to bring legal action against the government and the Roman Catholic Church to force them to hear me. I've worked so hard to remember, preparing and waiting for this day for many years.

I'm at a hotel in Duncan, BC. I knew that I wanted to have the hearing here, close to friends, but couldn't quite figure out why until Catherine, a good friend to my wife, commented that it was a good idea for it to be away from home, so the pain revealed at the hearing could be left behind and not be ever-present in a location I would see every day.

Sitting just inside the door at my right hand is my in-hearing support and elder Barney Williams. He's gone along this healing path before me and we have become close friends in the last few years. Immediately to his right is my lawyer. Directly across the table sits one of the adjudicators contracted by the federal government to hear and judge the various claims of abuse by residential school survivors. Beside her is the government lawyer.

The government lawyer and I met years ago during my working career with the Manitoba chiefs. She puts me at ease as we chat about past common experiences, and I feel I can trust her. Little do I know that we will not speak again in this room and that some of my anger will be directed at her as the representative of the Government of Canada.

Barney starts the hearing with prayers to the Creator in his language. He conducts a traditional smudging and healing ceremony that bestows guidance and protection. The cleansing smudge is feathered into our beings, our bodies, and fills the room. This goodness is spread with the strength of the eagle feather. He has asked and prayed for the kindness of all our departed friends and family through the grace of the Creator. It is time.

As with the government lawyer, I quickly become at ease with the adjudicator as she opens by talking about common interests and her knowledge of Manitoba. Her small stature and non-threatening approach help put me at ease. She reviews my personal information, including references to Mom and Dad, and the warm and proud memories I have of my family, grandparents and community. She speaks of the personal and professional highlights of my life.

As the morning progresses, she begins, little by little, asking questions about my abuse claims. My resolve to stay strong begins to evaporate as her comments and questions become more probing. I realize with a chill that this is not going to be as easy as I'd thought during my extensive preparation. I remember my older sister's shocked demeanour when she emerged from her hearing. I resolve that I will get through this. Although I tell myself that I have already gone through this and have still made a good life for myself, I feel myself weakening. I know that in my initial response and disclosure of abuse when my lawyer was preparing my claim, I barely acknowledged what I'd gone through as a young boy.

The adjudicator's questions become even more vivid and probing. The abuse I have endured in this particular incident has never been discussed except superficially, and never as graphically as in this moment. My anger and frustration must be obvious as I struggle to remain in my seat. I fight off a frantic urge to grab and slam the water jug, and whatever else is on the table, against the wall. In her wisdom, the adjudicator suggests that this would be a good time to have a break.

I'm overwhelmed by emotion and fear I'm having some kind of attack and will collapse before we're done. I push back from the table and stagger to my feet. The floodgates open and I try mightily to hold back tears and sobs.

Barney is standing beside me, helping me up and guiding me to the door. It opens to the waiting area; the bright daylight hits my eyes, and I reach for my wife as she flies from the waiting area to hold me in her arms. I can't envision how I look, and only realize later that this ordeal is nothing I have experienced before. It has touched my wife, her soul and consciousness, as deeply as it has mine.

She's frightened. Confronting this particular incident of abuse aloud has painted shock and horror all over me. My face is burning and I'm blind with tears. I'm shaking and falling. Never did I imagine that this hearing would create such panic in me.

In a moment, Mitzi, a support healer from the Tsow-Tun Le Lum Society, engulfs me and my wife in a comforting and caring embrace just a few feet from the now-open door of my hearing room. She directs us to a nearby private room. She sits directly in front of me and makes me focus on her eyes and on her words. She leads me in an empowering and strengthening ritual.

My emotions drain away with the last of my tears and I'm ready to continue fighting for the truth.

The hearing lasts for more than eight hours. We stop for a brief meal and forge on. The adjudicator questions me, clarifies what I'm saying, ensures precision. She is kind and thorough. I feel safe with her. No one else speaks. I tell her everything.

I know that evening has come, though the hearing room has no windows. I could go on for days with more detail, but I feel lighter now. The burdens in my mind and in my heart have been spoken aloud and their power over me broken. I look to Barney and he knows. It is enough.

I'm able to offer sincere thanks to the adjudicator and to the government lawyer. They have listened and they know. It is over.

The government lawyer steps forward. On behalf of the Government of Canada, she apologizes directly and wholeheartedly to me for the profoundly negative impact of my residential school experiences on my life.

Barney leads us in a prayerful ceremony, giving thanks to the Creator for the blessings of this day. He brushes me down from head to foot with an eagle-feather fan, so that my experiences are whisked away from me and left on the floor of that room. I've brought some stones from the ruins of the Fort Alexander Indian Residential School. They hold the essence of Canada's attempt to destroy my identity, and someday soon I'll return to that place to solidify my healing. Barney takes the stones from me and we both know that I've taken a huge step toward complete victory.

Someone once said that the hardest wounds to recognize and identify are those that go back to the distant past of our childhoods. We sometimes no longer remember the wounds, or who or what caused them. All that remains are the rigid behaviours and defensive reactions stirred up by the slightest offence. We continue to feel these childhood misfortunes at an unconscious level throughout our lives.

Personally, the fact that I forgive, to the best of my God-assisted ability, does not mean that I forget. I still see the wandering black shadow slithering across the dormitory. I still feel the wandering and groping hands of priests, brothers, teachers, supervisors and nuns. I still feel the knuckles. I still feel the sharp-toed boot, the grazing force of the billiard ball, the crack of the log on my back, the pangs of hunger and the fear of the night. While lying on my bed and praying, I seek to re-experience the manly, working smell of my father, the sad, kindly, soft face of my mother, and the warmth of the crackling fire in our family home. My life changed forever when I was seven years of age.

ACKNOWLEDGEMENTS

I extend my thanks to the following people.

To my dear friend and cousin Phil Fontaine—our discussions, talks and reminiscing through all the years of my life have lifted my spirit and been therapeutic for me. Your ability to recall details is extraordinary and has helped me to fill in many missing pieces.

To Rosa Walker and all the staff at the Indigenous Leadership Development Institute—your support, encouragement and love over the years have been invaluable.

To Barney (my elder) and Katrina Williams, and to Mitzi from Tsow-Tun Le Lum—you gave strength to me and to my wife during my hearing and afterward, helping me find my voice for my story.

To Tracey and the other therapists who helped me over the years—although we didn't travel to the depths of my experiences, you helped me begin to acknowledge that my experiences were real.

To my old schoolmates, my extended family and friends—we shared our journeys and supported each other with love and faith in each other.

To Father Guy Lavallee, for your support when I was a young boy at the Fort Alexander Indian Residential School while you were training there as a supervising assistant. You have enhanced the priesthood as you have become the spiritual leader you were meant to be. I treasure our friendship.

To those priests of St. Ignatius Parish in Winnipeg who have held my faith and trust for the last 28 years even during the most difficult days of remembering my experiences at residential school.

To Roger, one of my former bosses, who in his ignorance helped me to understand very clearly that the five-day-a-week boarding school he attended was an experience of privilege and not anything like the Indian residential schools I lived through.

To Phyllis, one of "two old dears in the map room" at Indian and Northern Affairs Canada in Winnipeg, and to Jackie at the Manitoba Map Sales office, for your patience, experience and professional help.

A very special thanks to Vivian Sinclair at Heritage House. You saw my dream and my yearning to help other survivors through telling my story, and made it possible through your unique interest, personal stewardship, expertise and commitment. You also understood and supported the vision that it would help Canadians understand the true intent and consequences of Indian residential schools in Canada.